How to Get Your School
MOVING and IMPROVING

How to Get Your School
MOVING and
IMPROVING

AN EVIDENCE-BASED APPROACH

Steve Dinham

ACER Press

First published 2008
by ACER Press, an imprint of
Australian Council *for* Educational Research Ltd
19 Prospect Hill Road, Camberwell
Victoria, 3124, Australia

Reprinted 2009 (Thrice), 2010

www.acerpress.com.au
sales@acer.edu.au

Text © Steve Dinham 2008
Design and typography © ACER Press 2008

This book is copyright. All rights reserved. Except under the conditions described in the *Copyright Act 1968* of Australia and subsequent amendments, and any exceptions permitted under the current statutory licence scheme administered by Copyright Agency Limited (www.copyright.com.au), no part of this publication may be reproduced, stored in a retrieval system, transmitted, broadcast or communicated in any form or by any means, optical, digital, electronic, mechanical, photocopying, recording or otherwise, without the written permission of the publisher.

Edited by Carolyn Glascodine
Cover design by mightyworld
Text design by Kerry Cooke, eggplant communications
Typeset by Kerry Cooke, eggplant communications
Printed in Australia by BPA Print Group
Cover photographs by Guy Lavoipierre. Thanks to Lalor North Primary School and Camberwell High School.

National Library of Australia Cataloguing-in-Publication data:

Author:	Dinham, Steve.
Title:	How to get your school moving and improving : an evidence-based approach / Steve Dinham.
Edition:	1st ed.
ISBN:	9780864319319 (pbk.)
Notes:	Includes index. Bibliography.
Subjects:	Educational leadership. School improvement programs. Effective teaching.
Dewey Number:	371.2011

Dedication

To Catherine, who has contributed significantly in many ways

Foreword

This is a very important book and it makes a significant contribution to the literature on school improvement, particularly the improvement of learning, teaching and leadership. It is especially significant for me in that Steve Dinham writes from a strong research agenda and much of this research has been conducted in Australian schools. How refreshing to have great home-grown evidence-based insights, wisdom and practical advice for educational practitioners that is not sourced only in the United States of America, the United Kingdom or New Zealand. Steve does acknowledge and report on key worldwide research, but only to complement his own work.

This is both a *personal* book (a research journey with personal and professional experiences of the author) and a *personalised* book (the author speaks directly to key educational stakeholders, especially teachers, educational leaders and policy makers). His frequent use of 'I' and his short cases and personal stories – vignettes and anecdotes – give the book a strong down-to-earth and practical flavour.

The author achieves a very important balance between research/theory and practical guidance and advice. In many ways the book bridges the theory–practice gap so often criticised by practitioners. He draws heavily on robust research, much of it his own (e.g. HSC, AESOP, the Teacher 2000 Project and QTAL) to develop our understanding of complex theoretical concepts, but presents these in an easy-to-read and concise form. He then expertly teases out the practical implications (guidelines and strategies) for teachers and other educational leaders. He also bridges the theory–practice gap by grounding himself, as a researcher/theoretician, in practice in schools as well as by encouraging practitioners involved in his research to be partners or co-researchers in his projects. This book can be regarded as a 'handbook' for both *understanding* (research evidence and attendant theories) and *doing* (practical strategies and advice), and it should prove to be a very valuable resource to a variety of educational stakeholders.

Steve certainly provides an important service to policy makers, teachers and other educational leaders in systems and schools insofar as he provides rich sources of very relevant research and literature in a user-friendly form. He uses the language of the practitioner just as much as he does the language of research and theory.

I am especially pleased to be able to read a book focusing, primarily, on what really matters in schools and schooling – the improvement of learning, teaching and leadership – and it is a great bonus for me that this is quintessentially an Australian tome. Its messages, however, are global and this book will be eagerly sought-after internationally.

I have commented generally on the book so far, but I would now like to highlight what I believe to be its specific strengths. I will pick out elements that especially resonate with me but there is so much richness in the book that no doubt you will have other favourite parts. I think that Steve's summary of what we know about student achievement, especially the key role of the quality teacher and quality teaching, gathers together in a small number of pages some powerful statements about the relationships between learning, teaching and leadership. I was especially impressed and pleasantly surprised by the evidence from his research to support the influential contribution of leaders, especially principals, to these relationships and their outcomes. A quote from Chapter 1 remains indelibly marked on my mind: '… school leaders can play major roles in creating the conditions in which teachers can teach effectively and students can learn, although the influence of leadership on student achievement has perhaps been underestimated' (p. 15). Later in the book he supports this view in his discussion and application of the 'Authoritative' approach to leadership.

I found Chapter 2 to be a stimulating and rewarding read. The discussion of the factors contributing to senior secondary teaching success is very valuable to teachers and all those who are engaged in promoting quality teachers and teaching (it has implications for those who prepare and professionally develop teachers). Most of the advice in this chapter, although specifically aimed at secondary teachers, has implications and applications for all teachers.

The evidence connecting principal leadership and exceptional student outcomes in Chapter 3 (from the cases in the AESOP study) is convincing and will add to our understanding of this complex set of relationships. The discussion and advice around the supporting model presented as Figure 3.1 should be compulsory reading for all educational leaders at all levels. This constitutes hard-hitting, direct advice that is again written with the practitioner in mind. It is a valuable resource for teachers and leaders.

The application of Baumrind's typology of parenting styles to leadership provided me with another way of thinking of leadership for improved teaching and learning. Steve's description, analysis and application of 'Authoritative leadership' to the leadership–learning–student outcomes dynamic makes a very useful contribution to unpacking and better understanding these relationships.

In the remainder of the book, I was especially informed and stimulated by the outcomes of the Teacher 2000 Project, especially the international comparative data, and the suggested strategies to enhance teacher satisfaction. His evidence on and insights into professional learning and building learning communities in practice, and making things happen through leadership of change will, I believe, prove to be essential reading for policy and decision makers in these areas. His final chapter on 'Looking back and moving forward' offers solid practical advice, derived from the evidence presented earlier in the book, for those charged with the awesome responsibility of getting their school or part of their school moving and improving.

This is a concise book which, given the busy life many educators lead, is a positive. Concise it may be, but it packs a lot of punch and is written in a forthright style. I strongly urge you to read it. You owe it to the precious children in our Australian schools.

Emeritus Professor Patrick Duignan
National President, Australian Council for Educational Leaders

Contents

	Foreword	*vi*
	Preface	*xi*
1	What we do know about student achievement?	1
	Introduction	1
	Schools *do* make a difference	1
	The teacher is *the* major in-school influence on student achievement	5
	How teacher expertise develops	7
	What works in teaching?	10
	Leadership also matters	15
	How people learn	16
2	Quality teaching in action	20
	Introduction	20
	Background to the NSW HSC study	20
	NSW HSC study	21
	Factors contributing to senior secondary teaching success	25
	Conclusion to discussion of the senior secondary successful teaching study	34
3	What effective school leaders do to promote teaching and learning	37
	Introduction	37
	Background to the AESOP study	38
	How the case study sites were selected	38
	How AESOP data were obtained and analysed	39
	How does leadership contribute to outstanding educational outcomes in junior secondary schooling?	42
	Conclusion to how school leaders promote teaching and learning	58

4	Responsive and demanding teaching and leadership	61
	Introduction	61
	Parenting styles	62
	Teaching and parenting styles	64
	Applying the typology to educational leadership	67
	Conclusion to discussion of educational leadership styles	72
	Education from the early 1960s to today: Where we went wrong	73
5	Teacher and school executive satisfaction, motivation and stress	80
	Introduction	80
	Context of teacher satisfaction	80
	The Teacher 2000 Project	82
	Implications of the teacher satisfaction research	90
	Strategies to enhance teacher satisfaction	92
6	The importance of professional learning: Building a learning community	101
	Introduction	101
	Traditional and emerging approaches to teacher professional learning	101
	Background: The individual teacher, school effectiveness and learning communities	103
	Case studies of learning communities in practice	105
	Drawing from the case studies: How does a learning community develop and sustain itself?	111
	Implications and conclusions	113
7	Making change happen and keeping it going	119
	Introduction	119
	The nature of change	119
	Groupthink and Balkanisation	121
	Overcoming resistance to change	124
	Importance of school culture	129
	Managing conflict and change	133
8	Looking back and moving forward	138
	Putting it all together: How educational leaders get schools moving and improving	139

Preface

To speak in a manner intelligible to the multitude, and to comply with every general custom that does not hinder the attainment of our purpose ... we shall in this way gain a friendly audience for the reception of the truth.

(Spinoza)

Welcome to this book.

How to Get Your School Moving and Improving is a distillation of much of what I've learned about student learning and achievement, teaching, teachers, schools and leadership over my career. I was a teacher for 14 years before becoming involved with teacher education, and I spent 18 years working with undergraduate and postgraduate education students and the wider profession. I moved to my present position at the Australian Council for Educational Research in 2007 and I'm still very much involved with teachers' professional learning through short courses, conferences, workshops, research, doctoral supervision and my own writing.

Over the past 20 years I've been part of many research projects across the broad areas of student achievement, quality teaching, educational leadership, educational change, teachers' work and lives, teachers' professional learning, professional teaching standards, teacher recognition and teacher career structures.

In this book I draw upon many of the findings from that work and the work of others that has helped shape my knowledge and understanding of the field. I have tried to make what I have to say concise, relevant and useful, because I know how busy educators are with their day-to-day work. My philosophy on educational research is that it needs to be *Rigorous*, *Relevant* and *Readable* – my 'three Rs of research' – if it's to be influential in schools, and I've tried to adhere to that in my research and with what is presented in this book.[1] I have also included the voices and stories of educators and students who have contributed to the studies, along with short case studies and vignettes to add detail, richness and authenticity.

My aim has been to speak directly to anyone interested and involved with school leadership and improvement – 'to speak in a manner intelligible to the multitude' – to assist them to understand what they are doing, and what they can do, in order to make things happen in their school. In all of this, there is a focus on students and student achievement and a major emphasis on evidence – to cut through the clouds of fashion, fad, jargon and ideology that frequently surround education – to show what research has revealed about what really works and adds value in schools.

I know that many educators are suspicious of 'research' and 'theory', in some cases for good reason, so let me reassure you that the studies I have incorporated in this book involved many teachers from many schools and systems across a variety of countries. The research findings have been 'road-tested' and met with approval in the more than 300 presentations I have made in every Australian state and territory and in countries such as New Zealand, the United Kingdom, Sweden, Crete, the United States of America and Canada.

At the end of each chapter there are references to provide support for what I'm saying and to assist those who wish to learn more about the various studies, especially more detailed information on relevant literature and methodology.

Much of the work in the chapters that follow was carried out with fellow researchers and educators and I thank them for their contribution to my understanding. I've also had the pleasure of working with and supervising postgraduate research students at three universities, examined research dissertations for a wide range of universities and reviewed articles for leading international journals. Every year, every project and every professional activity leads to a little more understanding. Looking back, I wish I had known more of what I know now when I was searching for answers earlier in my career, but that's the nature of experience, expertise and life. I'm happy to share with you my current thinking about what I've managed to find out.

I hope this book meets your needs as you seek to grow professionally and to improve teaching and learning in your setting, whatever the stage of your career, whatever your role, and wherever you work. Context is important and so I would suggest that you treat what you encounter in this book as guidelines and frameworks for reflection, planning, action and evaluation, rather than non-negotiable recipes or prescriptions. There are no quick fixes, although there are likely to be some things that you would like to change or implement immediately.

You, along with your colleagues, need to reflect on, adapt and apply what is known about quality teaching, student learning and school improvement to your particular school or setting, rather than simply hope to copy what has worked for others in another time and place.

In presenting what I have in this way, I hope to 'gain a friendly audience for the reception of the truth'.

My best wishes for the success of this process.

Steve Dinham

Notes
1. Dinham, S. (2007). Educational Research and the 'Three R's'. *Education Review*, *17*(2), 16–18.

1 | What do we know about student achievement?

Learning is not attained by chance. It must be sought for with ardour and attended to with diligence.

(Abigail Adams)

Introduction

This chapter begins with an examination of what should be the focus of every school, every educational system and every education department or faculty of education – student learning and achievement.

Changing views on the effect that schools and teachers have on student achievement are examined, and current international research findings on what actually adds value in schooling are considered.

What we know about the development of teacher expertise is also explored. An overview on leadership and how it can influence teaching and learning is then provided, which serves as a foundation for later chapters.

I conclude this chapter with an overview of research evidence on learning from the excellent publication *How people learn* from the US National Research Council.[1] *How to get your school moving and improving* is intentionally more about teaching and leadership than learning, but I think you will be able to make the connection between the two through the use of this overview.

Schools *do* make a difference

Streaming and categorisation of students: Social-biological determinism

The mid-1960s may seem a long time ago, but in the development of our thinking about teaching and learning, this period is both significant and comparatively recent.

Up until the mid-1960s, the prevailing view was that schools made almost no difference to student achievement. What students could achieve in their education was largely predetermined by heredity, where they lived, their socio-economic background and family circumstances. Measured 'IQ' was considered a powerful predictor of student achievement and seen as largely innate and fixed by the time young people got to school. In other words, every student had his or her personal glass ceiling when it came to educational attainment. More than this, whole schools, suburbs, cultural groups and even regions were consigned to a particular category and likely future in society, with expectations for achievement and probable employment adjusted accordingly. Students who didn't fit this pattern, for example young people from very poor areas with high measured IQ, were seen as the exception that proved the rule for most of their peers. It was very hard to escape this social categorisation and, as we shall see, one of the most damaging things we can do to people is to put them into categories and treat them accordingly.

In the United States of America and beyond, a very influential publication of the time was the so-called 'Coleman Report' of 1966, *Equality of educational opportunity*, which concluded that the quality of schooling was responsible for only about 10 per cent of the variance in student achievement.[2] The powerful conclusion drawn from this study was that schools could exert only a small influence on student accomplishment.[3] Many people today, including practising teachers, still subscribe, consciously or subconsciously, to various forms of biological-social determinism, despite overwhelming evidence to the contrary.

This view that schools made little or no difference was reflected in the nature of schools themselves, with public 'junior' high schools (and some systemic religious schools) providing various forms of 'technical' education for children of the working classes prior to them entering lower-skilled occupations and trades.

Girls in these schools studied various 'domestic science' (cooking, sewing) and clerical subjects (bookkeeping, typing) while boys undertook 'blue collar' subjects in woodwork, metalwork and technical drawing to prepare them for trades and semi-skilled labour. Many such schools were single-sex, which both reflected and reinforced stereotypes about careers for working-class boys and girls.

In contrast, more affluent areas were served by government and private 'full' secondary schools, which were geared to preparation for 'white collar' work, university entrance and the professions. Although not as powerful as in the United Kingdom, the 'class system' of the time in Australia was important in determining people's life chances. (Though diminished, these influences are still strong today.)

Students tended to be streamed into one of these broad pathways at the end of primary school or even earlier. Some gifted students from poorer backgrounds who passed special examinations were offered the chance to attend the 'better' primary and secondary schools. In reality, however, most students and their families had little say – the decision was made for them by circumstances and the expectations for them held by others. Where students were able to escape this broad social categorisation and streaming, this often required determination and sacrifice from parents and long-distance commuting from students. Those students who emerged from the junior 'technical' highs and who aspired to university study and the professions were faced with long years of 'night school' or correspondence study, and lowly paid on-the-job education in accounting firms, legal offices and the like, to bridge the gap.

In Australia, reflecting earlier developments in the United States of America, the United Kingdom and similar nations, this situation started to change in the 1960s.

Comprehensive education

The first key change was the provision of (near) universal 'comprehensive' education through a single model of secondary education. The playing field still wasn't level, but some of the hills had been lowered, and this change at least made it possible for more young people to choose to study from the same range of subjects as students from 'better' areas and schools. They could now complete their secondary education at their local secondary school, although in reality, in the less affluent areas only a small minority managed to complete post-compulsory education under these new arrangements. In more isolated areas, completing secondary school was still difficult and usually required boarding or commuting to complete the final years of high school (and still does today for some students in isolated areas).

To use myself and New South Wales as a case study, I entered public high school in a south-western suburb of Sydney in 1966, the year decimal currency was introduced to Australia. Without knowing it at the time, I was benefiting from the 'Wyndham Scheme', the new form of comprehensive education introduced in 1962 under the leadership of Sir Harold Wyndham, Director-General of Education in NSW. Coincidentally, almost 40 years later I received the Sir Harold Wyndham Medal from the Australian College of Educators but I can assure you that I certainly wasn't thinking along those lines in 1966. Both my parents had left school after 'third form' (now Year 9) with the 'Intermediate Certificate', and six years of high school seemed daunting to me and many of my peers. Like so many young people from similar backgrounds, there were no role models for either completing secondary school or undertaking tertiary study. This was unfamiliar territory.

The new NSW Higher School Certificate (HSC) was awarded for the first time in 1967 to the first 'sixth form' classes (now Year 12). It was based on six years of secondary study (four years for the School Certificate and another two years for the Higher School Certificate), rather than the previous model of five years (three years for the Intermediate and another two years for the Leaving Certificate). Final results were still determined by external public examinations.

Students could still leave school at 15, however, and many did as 15 was the traditional age to enter apprenticeships, although increasingly, those who left school early now did so after Year 10 at 16 with the School Certificate.

The HSC was now the means for determining university entry, although only 20 per cent of students who had begun high school in 1962 completed the first HSC examinations in 1967, and university fees and a lack of family role models no doubt still deterred many students from attending university. (As will be seen later, a teacher's scholarship was important in some of these school leavers gaining a tertiary education, especially women.) Overall, fewer than half of those who completed the inaugural HSC of 1967 entered university in the following year, but this situation would change.

These patterns and developments were mirrored in other Australian jurisdictions as the 'baby boomers' moved through schooling, and post-compulsory retention and the numbers of those entering tertiary education increased. Many of those who entered colleges and universities were first generation tertiary students, as I was. In Australia, the abolition of university fees in the early 1970s was also a significant factor in increased tertiary participation, although this incentive was undermined somewhat by the introduction of higher education 'contribution' fees and loans in later decades.

School effectiveness research

The second broad change influencing our thinking about student achievement came from school effectiveness research, largely from North America. In the post Second World War period, the United States of America had invested heavily in education; education was seen as vital to equity, opportunity and the economic health of the nation.

However, there was increasing concern about the varying performance of students, especially those in large urban secondary schools where considerable funds had been expended in the hope of improving opportunity and achievement. When 'like' schools were compared, despite similar clientele, resources, curricula and administration, some schools were clearly more successful than others when it came to student performance on standardised measures. Whatever was responsible for this disparity, it wasn't just the students, and it wasn't just resources.

To investigate school performance, 'input–output' economic studies were carried out from the mid-1960s to the early 1970s, and were accompanied later by 'effective school' studies (early to late 1970s), which led to 'school improvement' studies (late 1970s to mid-1980s) and more recently, 'context variables' studies (late 1980s to the present).[4]

Rather than performance being largely determined by the 'raw materials' – the students, resources and structures – other more intangible and contextual factors were clearly at work. While attention was focused for a time at the school level – including the influence of leadership, which we will return to later – as researchers began to 'drill down', it was becoming apparent that student achievement also varied considerably *within* seemingly successful schools, and in fact within all schools. It was found that the differences within schools were actually greater than the overall differences in student achievement *between* schools. (This phenomenon remains true in most schools to this day.)

From the 1970s, the attention of some researchers turned more to what was happening within individual classrooms.

By the late 1980s, the belief that schools, and by implication teachers, made no difference to student achievement had been powerfully refuted.

In fact, in the United States of America, the view that schools *do* make a difference has been cast in legislation with the *No Child Left Behind Act* of 2001, which doesn't just acknowledge that schools make a difference, but mandates that they have to, with consequences if they don't.

The teacher is *the* major in-school influence on student achievement

As work continued on effective schools and successful teaching and the corpus of completed research studies grew, the evidence was mounting that not only did schools make a difference, but that the teacher was the major in-school influence on student achievement.

An important innovation was the application of the technique of meta-analysis to these burgeoning studies. Meta-analysis is essentially the analysis of existing analyses, and was developed from earlier approaches by Gene Glass in the 1970s.

> Meta-analysis refers to the analysis of analyses. I use it to refer to the statistical analysis of a large collection of results from individual studies for the purpose of integrating the findings. It connotes a rigorous alternative

to the casual, narrative discussions of research studies which typify our attempts to make sense of the rapidly expanding research literature.[5]

Today, meta-analysis is the foundation for analysing studies of teacher effectiveness, with 'effect size' a key unit of measurement.

A meta-analysis combines the results from a number of studies to determine the average effect of a given technique. When conducting a meta-analysis, a researcher translates the results of a given study into a unit of measurement referred to as an effect size. An effect size expresses the increase or decrease in achievement of the experimental group (the group of students who are exposed to a specific instructional technique) in standard deviation units.[6]

We will consider effect sizes for different teaching techniques and aspects of teaching shortly.

Major sources of variance in student achievement

- What then are the main influences on student achievement?
- How can we explain the variance in students' performance?

In answering these questions, I draw heavily on the important work of Professor John Hattie from the University of Auckland, New Zealand.[7]

As a result of a meta-analysis of many thousands of studies, Hattie and his colleagues found six major sources of variance. It should be pointed out that these factors explain or account for a proportion of the *variance* in student achievement, not the proportion of the actual marks or scores achieved by students (a common misconception).

- *Students:* account for about 50% of the variance of achievement: 'It is what students bring to the table that predicts achievement more than any other variable'.
- *Home:* accounts for about 5–10% of the variance: 'the major effects of the home are already accounted for by the attributes of the student. The home effects are more related to the levels of expectation and encouragement, and certainly not a function of the involvement of the parents or caregivers in the management of schools'.
- *School:* accounts for about 5–10% of the variance: 'the finances, the school size, the class size, the buildings are important as they must be there in some form for a school to exist, but that is about it'.
- *Principals:* 'are already accounted for in the variance attributed to schools; their effect is mainly indirect through their influence on school climate and culture'. [As will be seen later, I think that the influence of principals and leadership generally may have been underestimated, at least in successful schools.]

- *Peer effects:* account for 5–10% of the variance: 'It does not matter too much who you go to school with, and when students are taken from one school and put in another the influence of peers is minimal (of course, there are exceptions, but they do not make the norm)'.
- *Teachers:* account for about 30% of variance: 'It is what teachers know, do, and care about which is very powerful in this learning equation'.[8]

There is now considerable and incontrovertible international evidence that the major in-school influence on student achievement is the quality of the classroom teacher.[9]

> ... the most important factor affecting student learning is the teacher ... The immediate and clear implication of this finding is that seemingly more can be done to improve education by improving the effectiveness of teachers than by any other single factor.[10]

However, research evidence is also clear on some related matters. Firstly, it takes time, learning and effort to develop from a novice to an 'expert' teacher, and not all teachers become experts. Secondly, teacher expertise varies considerably.[11]

How teacher expertise develops

Work on the development of teacher expertise is a sub-set of work on expertise generally. It has been found that it takes around eight to ten years to become expert at anything, child prodigies aside.

In the 1980s, Hubert and Stuart Dreyfus developed a five-stage model of the activities involved in skills acquisition which proved popular and has since gone through various iterations.[12] Dreyfus and Dreyfus drew on cases from foreign language acquisition, learning to play chess and flight instruction. The five stages or levels of skills acquisition in their initial model were identified as:

1. Novice
2. Competence
3. Proficiency
4. Expertise
5. Mastery

Dreyfus and Dreyfus were concerned with four key mental functions performed by practitioners:

1. *Recollection:* which ranges from Non-situational (Novice) to Situational (Master)
2. *Recognition:* Decomposed (Novice) to Holistic (Master)

3 *Decision:* Analytical (Novice) to Intuitive (Master)
4 *Awareness:* Monitoring (Novice) to Absorbed (Master)

Overall, the behaviour of novices tends to be rule governed, while the behaviour of experts/masters tends to be governed mainly by personal and professional knowledge. Novice chess players think about rules and simple moves, while experts who know the rules think more about complex strategies involving many potential moves and their consequences.

Experts/masters tend to be skilled at reading context and noticing detail, while novices barely notice detail and context and how it all fits together.

Novices need structure, while experts or masters need autonomy, and find rules and structure inhibiting. The implication is that it is a mistake to treat a novice like an expert or master, and vice versa.

The National Research Council of the United States of America provided the following distinguishing characteristics for experts:[13]

1 Experts notice features and meaningful patterns of information that novices do not notice.
2 Experts have acquired a great deal of content knowledge that is organised in ways that reflect a deep understanding of their subject matter.
3 Experts' knowledge cannot be reduced to sets of isolated facts or propositions but, instead, reflects contexts of applicability; that is, the knowledge is 'conditionalised' on a set of circumstances.
4 Experts are able to flexibly retrieve important aspects of their knowledge with little attentional effort.
5 Although experts know their disciplines thoroughly, this does not guarantee that they are able to teach others.
6 Experts have varying levels of flexibility in their approach to new situations.

Similar findings have been found for 'expert teachers'. John Hattie and Dick Jaeger identified five major dimensions of excellent teachers, underpinned by 16 prototypic attributes:[14]

A   *Can identify essential representations of their subject(s)*
A1 Expert teachers have deeper representations about teaching and learning.
A2 Expert teachers adopt a problem-solving stance towards their work.
A3 Expert teachers can anticipate, plan and improvise as required by the situation.
A4 Expert teachers are better decision-makers and can identify which decisions are important and which are less important.

B   *Guiding learning through classroom interactions*
B5   Expert teachers are proficient at creating an optimal classroom climate for learning.
B6   Expert teachers have a multidimensionally complex perception of classroom situations.
B7   Expert teachers are more context-dependent and have high situation cognition.

C   *Monitoring learning and provide feedback*
C8   Expert teachers are more adept at monitoring student problems and assessing their level of understanding and progress, and they provide much more relevant, useful feedback.
C9   Expert teachers are more adept at developing and testing hypotheses about learning difficulties or instructional strategies.
C10   Expert teachers are more automatic.

D   *Attending to affective attributes*
D11   Expert teachers have high respect for students.
D12   Expert teachers are passionate about teaching and learning.

E   *Influencing student outcomes*
E13   Expert teachers engage students in learning, and develop in their students' self-regulation, involvement in mastery learning, enhanced self-efficacy and self-esteem as learners.
E14   Expert teachers provide adequate challenging tasks and goals for students.
E15   Expert teachers have positive influences on their students' achievement.
E16   Expert teachers enhance surface and deep learning.

It needs to be emphasised that progression from novice to expert is neither automatic nor merely the result of accumulated experience. Further, being an expert is not a matter of being a 'born teacher' either (there is no such thing),[15] or of personality, intelligence, memory or some form of general ability.

While attaining expert teacher status can take a substantial amount of time, this is more a matter of 'rich' experience, working and talking with colleagues and supervisors, professional learning, trial and error and experimentation, role-modelling, feedback and reflection.

There is a saying that while some teachers have 25 years of experience, other teachers have the same year of experience 25 times over. In other words, not all teachers will reach expert status and none will do so automatically. However, all teachers are capable of learning to be more effective, including highly experienced and even 'stale' teachers, as we will see in later chapters.

David Berliner is an authority in the field of the development of teaching expertise. In reviewing the research literature, including his own work, he concluded:[16]

> Experts in teaching share characteristics of experts in more prestigious fields such as chess, medical diagnosis, and physics problem solving. Thus, there is no basis to believe that there are differences in the sophistication of the cognitive processes used by teachers and experts in other fields. This is an important conclusion for educators who are generally held in low esteem by the public.

In considering how long it takes to develop expertise in teaching, Berliner concluded that moving from novice status to achieving competence as a teacher takes around two to three years. The development of a high level of skill, however, takes five to seven years and a great deal of work.[17]

In Chapter 2, we will consider the findings from a study of successful senior secondary teachers, but first, it is necessary to disaggregate what research has revealed about the effects of various factors, strategies and interventions on student achievement.

What works in teaching?

As mentioned previously, there is now a large international research literature on student achievement. The technique of meta-analysis enables us to combine and integrate the findings from many studies.

Robert Marzano, in a very useful text worth seeking out, has summarised the major factors affecting student achievement:[18]

Table 1.1 Major factors affecting student achievement

Factor	Example
School	Guaranteed and viable curriculum
	Challenging goals and effective feedback
	Parent and community involvement
	Safe and orderly environment
	Collegiality and professionalism
Teacher	Instructional strategies
	Classroom management
	Classroom curriculum design
Student	Home atmosphere
	Learned intelligence and background knowledge
	Motivation

To help us to 'unpack' this further, John Hattie has provided a comprehensive list of 100 influences on student achievement based on more than 700 meta-analyses containing over 50,000 studies.[19] Space precludes a detailed examination, but calculated effect sizes for the broad categories of teacher, curricula, teaching, student, home and school, revealed the following. Generally, an effect size (ES) less than 0.2 is considered weak or insignificant, 0.2–<0.4 is small, 0.4–<0.6 is moderate, and an effect size of 0.6 or above is considered large, although ES can be calculated and reported in slightly different ways. (Some texts, for example, give a large effect size as being 0.8 or more.)

Table 1.2 Effect sizes of factors affecting student achievement

Category	Effect size
Teacher	.50
Curricula	.45
Teaching	.43
Student	.39
Home	.35
School	.23
Average	.40

To disaggregate these findings, Hattie's 'top 20' influences on student achievement from his list of 100 are as follows:

Table 1.3 Top 20 influences on student achievement

Rank	Category	Influence	Effect size
1	Student	Self-report grades	1.44
2	Teacher	Absence of disruptive students	.86
3	Teacher	Classroom behaviour	.80
4	Teacher	Quality of teaching	.77
5	Teaching	Reciprocal teaching	.74
6	Student	Prior achievement	.73
7	Teacher	Teacher–student relationships	.72
8	Teacher	Feedback	.72
9	Teacher	Providing formative evaluation to teachers	.70
10	Teaching	Creativity programs	.70
11	Teaching	Teaching students self-verbalisation	.67
12	Teaching	Meta-cognition strategies	.67

13	Curricula	Reading: vocabulary programs	.67
14	Curricula	Reading: repeated reading programs	.67
15	Teacher	Teacher professional development on student achievement	.64
16	Teaching	Teaching problem solving	.61
17	School	Acceleration of gifted	.60
18	Teaching	Study skills	.59
19	Teaching	Time on task	.59
20	Teaching	Direct instruction	.59

The above list highlights yet again the importance of the classroom teacher and quality teaching. In considering Hattie's overall list of 100 influences and effect sizes for these, a number of conclusions can be drawn:

- The teacher and the quality of his or her teaching are major influences on student achievement, along with the individual student and his or her prior achievement (all have large effect sizes).
- School-based influences (beyond the classroom) have weaker effects on student achievement.
- Structural and organisational arrangements (open vs. traditional classrooms; multi-age vs. age graded classes; ability grouping; gender; class size; mainstreaming) have negligible or small effects on student learning. It is the quality of teaching that occurs within these structural arrangements that is important.
- Examples of 'active teaching' (reciprocal teaching; feedback; teaching self-verbalisation; meta-cognition strategies; direct instruction; mastery learning; testing) have large to moderate effects on student achievement.
- Effect sizes are negligible or small for facilitatory teaching (simulations and games; inquiry-based teaching; individualised instruction; problem-based learning; differentiated teaching for boys and girls; web-based learning; whole language reading; inductive teaching).
- Strategies to promote and remediate literacy figure prominently in Hattie's full list. Literacy is the foundation of student achievement.[20]
- While socio-economic status and home environment do have an effect on student achievement (each ranked = 22nd on Hattie's list with an ES of .57), this influence is outweighed by the quality of teaching (ES = .77) students receive in the classroom.
- Overall, the quality of the teacher and the quality of teaching (large effect sizes) are much more important than structural or working conditions (negligible or small effect sizes), demonstrating the futility and waste of 'fiddling around the

edges' of schooling without sufficiently addressing the quality of teachers and the quality of teaching within schools and classrooms.

It is because of findings like these that there has been so much attention paid to improving teacher education, the quality of teachers[21] and the quality of teaching in recent times.[22]

However, it must be recognised that there is still not a level playing field either in education or in life, and I can't see that changing much. Schooling still reflects and reinforces many social and economic divisions, and students after all, spend less than 15 per cent of their time in school. Socio-economic status and family background still exert a powerful influence, not on innate student ability or capacity, but on expectations, support, opportunities and life choices.

In the highest performing nations, however, socio-economic factors have less influence on student achievement than in Australia, once again pointing to the importance of quality teaching rather than innate ability. In a paper for the Business Council of Australia, Lawrence Ingvarson, Elizabeth Kleinhenz and I noted:[23]

> *Although Australia performs well on international measures of student achievement such as PISA (the OECD's Programme for International Student Assessment involving 400,000 15-year-olds in 57 countries), there are concerns over equity. Many students in Australia continue to struggle, including Indigenous students, where the performance gap with non-Indigenous students remains wide. Students' social backgrounds have a greater influence on educational results in Australia than in higher performing countries such as Finland and Canada.*[24]

Dangers and harm of categorisation

One of the most harmful things we can do to a child is to categorise him or her as a particular type of person or learner. I have seen classrooms in which students as young as eight have been 'tested' to determine their 'learning style' and are labelled, and label themselves, according to this type – 'I'm a … learner', 'I can do …', 'I'm no good at …', etc.

Any time we categorise students there are certain consequences:

1. There is a necessity to define the group and explain how membership will be determined – who is in and who is out. This can be quite arbitrary and differences between groups and individuals tend to be exaggerated to make the 'case'.
2. There is a need to justify the existence of the group and to defend its existence, i.e. why and how the group is 'different'.

3 Members of the group then inevitably receive 'special' treatment while others miss out.
4 Members are usually told of their membership or 'label', which encourages entity thinking: 'gifted' (see Scott, 2008[25]), 'disadvantaged', 'learning difficulties', male, 'left-brain', 'kinaesthetic', i.e. 'I'm a ... learner', 'I'm a ... type of personality', and so forth, setting up a self-fulfilling prophecy, rather than adopting an incremental approach to learning and development.
5 Catering to a particular perceived 'learning style' reinforces that style (ironically, learning styles are *learned*, not innate) at the expense of other approaches.
6 Those so labelled (and frequently their families) see the role of teachers and others as *recognising* their particular abilities, rather than *developing* their capacities further, which they see as fixed.
7 Labelling based on stereotypes (e.g. boys, girls) then reinforces those stereotypes.

By all means meet the needs of young people, challenge them and enrich their learning through exposure to a variety of learning opportunities; just don't categorise them and limit their horizons through making them believe they are a particular fixed type of learner or person. Categorisation of students is another form of streaming.

The research evidence is clear that categorising learners and catering for supposed differences has a very weak effect (ES) on learning, as demonstrated by Hattie's work.[26] Rather than limiting young people's horizons in this way, I believe that with good teaching, it is possible to teach almost anybody almost anything.

These issues aside, schooling and education remain our best chance for changing people's lives and society for the better. The data on all sorts of social and economic indicators and outcomes correlate strongly with educational achievement. For example, the higher people's level of educational attainment, the higher their income, health and life expectancy, on average.

The best thing we can do for any young person is to provide them with a quality education. Intellectual capacity is not fixed and can be increased through education. Measured IQ has steadily risen over the past century – the so-called 'Flynn Effect'[27] – to the extent that IQ tests have to be periodically normalised so that the average score remains at 100. Young people are becoming smarter over generations, and the major factor behind the almost universal rise in measured IQ is schooling, with health and nutrition also playing their part. Parental literacy, an outcome of schooling, also plays an important role.[28]

Leadership also matters

We have confirmed the crucial importance of the teacher to student learning. The challenge for any educational leader, and the focus of this book, is to make things happen within individual classrooms. This matter is taken up in greater detail in later chapters but overall, *school leaders can play major roles in creating the conditions in which teachers can teach effectively and students can learn*, although the influence of leadership on student achievement has perhaps been underestimated.[29]

Today, leadership is seen as central and essential to delivering the changes, improvement and performance that society increasingly expects of all organisations, including schools. Because of this perceived importance, leadership has been the subject of widespread in-depth study and popular writing. The shelves of airport bookshops are filled with the latter.

What has become clear is that leadership, including educational leadership, is a more contentious, complex, situated and dynamic phenomenon than previously thought.

The study of leadership has been through many phases and fashions, with various idealistic, empirical, theoretical and ideological stances: trait versus process leadership; assigned versus emergent leadership; bureaucratic versus charismatic leadership; administration/management versus leadership; transactional versus transformation leadership; universal versus contextual/contingent leadership; 'born' versus 'learned' leadership; command versus relationships; line management versus distributed leadership, and so forth.[30]

Part of the confusion has been caused by the conflation of *leaders* (their attributes, knowledge and skills, i.e. entities) with *leadership* (the influence exercised by and the functions performed by leaders, i.e. behaviours and processes).

As noted, the prevailing view until the mid-1960s was that leaders and schools had very little influence on student achievement. Now, however, the pressure is on school leaders to be leaders of learning and not just managers or administrators, and for teaching and learning to be the prime focus of the school. (I know this sounds a strange thing to have to say, but the reality is that during the fixation with school management that occurred during the late 1980s–1990s, teachers, teaching and students barely rated a mention in in-service courses for school leaders. It felt wrong to me at the time and still does.)

While the administrative and management functions of the school leader are important and are not going to go away, and many would argue are increasing due to increased responsibilities and accountability, leaders need to find the time and means to focus on improving the quality of teaching and learning within their schools. Evidence on how this can be achieved will be provided in the following chapters. (I should point out that when I use the term 'school leader', unless stated otherwise, I am considering principals, deputies, others holding formal leadership positions in schools and teacher leadership beyond the classroom – not only principals.)

How people learn

Two valuable publications under the umbrella *How people learn* were published in the late 1990s and resulted from the work of the Committee on Developments in the Science of Learning under the auspices of the National Research Council of the United States of America.[31] I recommend these texts to any educator interested in understanding learning and teaching, and who wishes to distinguish research evidence about learning and teaching from the fashions, fantasies, superstitions and ideological claptrap that frequently confronts and confuses us.

As *How to get your school moving and improving* is on balance more about teaching than learning, I've included this summary to act as a framework for reflection and comparison with what I have provided in this book. I believe the two are highly congruent, given the emphasis within each on evidence, but then I wouldn't recommend *How people learn* if I didn't think it supported my case.

Key findings from how people learn

1 Students come to the classroom with preconceptions about how the world works. If their initial understanding is not engaged, they may fail to grasp the new concepts and information that are taught, or they may learn them for the purposes of a test but revert to the preconceptions outside the classroom.
2 To develop competence in an area of enquiry, students must:
   (a) have a deep foundation of factual knowledge
   (b) understand facts and ideas in the context of a conceptual framework
   (c) organise knowledge in ways that facilitate retrieval and application.
3 A 'metacognitive' approach to instruction can help students learn to take control of their own learning by defining learning goals and monitoring their progress in achieving them.

Implications for teaching
1 Teachers must draw out and work with students' pre-existing understandings.
2 Teachers must teach some subject matter in depth, providing many examples in which the same concept is at work and providing a firm foundation of factual knowledge.
3 The teaching of metacognitive skills should be integrated into the curriculum in a variety of subject areas.

Designing classroom environments
1 Schools and classrooms must be learner-centred.
2 To provide a knowledge-centred classroom environment, attention must be given to what is taught (information, subject matter), why it is taught (understanding), and what competence or mastery looks like.
3 Formative assessments – ongoing assessments designed to make students' thinking visible to both teachers and students – are central. They permit the teacher to grasp the students' preconceptions, understand where the students are in the 'developmental corridor' from informal to formal thinking and design instruction accordingly. In the assessment-centred classroom environment, formative assessments help both teachers and students monitor progress.
4 Learning is influenced in fundamental ways by the context in which it takes place. A community-centred approach requires the development of norms for the classroom and school, as well as connections to the outside world, that support core learning values.

Applying the design framework to adult learning
Many approaches to teaching adults consistently violate principles for optimising learning. Professional development programs for teachers, for example, frequently:

- are not learner-centred
- are not knowledge-centred
- are not assessment-centred
- are not community-centred.[32]

In Chapter 2 we will now explore the 'how' aspects of improving teaching and learning, drawing on the findings from one study.

Notes
1 Bransford, J., Brown, A., & Cocking, R. (Eds.). (2000). *How people learn: Brain, mind, experience, and school*. Washington, DC: National Academy Press; Donovan, M., Bransford, J., & Pellegrino, J. (Eds.). (1999). *How people learn: Bridging research and practice*. Washington, DC: National Academy Press.

2 'An important technique for analysing the effect of categorical factors on a response is to perform an analysis of variance. An ANOVA decomposes the variability in the response variable amongst the different factors. Depending upon the type of analysis, it may be important to determine: (a) which factors have a significant effect on the response, and/or (b) how much of the variability in the response variable is attributable to each factor.' http://www.statgraphics.com/analysis_of_variance.htm
3 Marzano, R., Pickering, D., & Pollock, J. (2005). *Classroom instruction that works: Research-based strategies for increasing student achievement.* Upper Saddle River, NJ: Pearson.
4 Reynolds, D., Teddlie, C., Creemers, B., Scheerens, J., & Townsend, T. (2000). An introduction to school effectiveness research. In Teddlie, C., & Reynolds, D. (Eds.). *The international handbook of school effectiveness research* (pp. 3–25). London: Falmer.
5 Glass, G. V. (1976). Primary, secondary, and meta-analysis of research. *Educational Researcher, 5*, 3–8, p. 3.
6 Marzano, Pickering, & Pollock (2005). p. 4.
7 Hattie, J. (2003). Teachers make a difference: What is the research evidence? Paper presented at the ACER Annual Conference, October. http://www.leadspace.govt.nz/leadership/articles/teachers-make-a-difference.php
8 Hattie (2003). pp. 1–2.
9 Organisation for Economic Co-operation and Development. (2005). *Teachers matter: Attracting, developing and retaining effective teachers.* Paris: Author.
10 Wright, S., Horn, S., & Sanders, W. (1997). Teacher and classroom context effects on student achievement: Implications for teacher evaluation. *Journal of Personnel Evaluation in Education, 11*, 57–67, p. 63.
11 Darling-Hammond, L. (2006). *Powerful teacher education.* San Francisco: Jossey-Bass.
12 Dreyfus, S., & Dreyfus, H. (1980). *A five-stage model of the mental activities involved in directed skills acquisition.* (pp. 1–18). Operations Research Center, University of California, Berkeley.
13 Bransford, J., Brown, A., & Cocking, R. (Eds.). (2000). *How people learn* (p. 31). Washington, DC: National Academy Press.
14 In Hattie (2003), pp. 5–9.
15 Scott, C., & Dinham, S. (2008). Born not made: The nativist myth and teachers' thinking. *Teacher Development, 12*(2), 127–136.
16 Berliner, D. (2004). Describing the behaviour and documenting the accomplishments of expert teachers. *Bulletin of Science, Technology & Society, 24*(3), 200–212, p. 63.
17 Berliner (2004). p. 201.
18 Marzano, R. (2003). *What works in schools: Translating research into action.* Alexandria, VA: ASCD, p. 10.
19 Hattie, J. (2007). *Developing potentials for learning: Evidence, assessment, and progress.* EARLI Biennial Conference, Budapest, Hungary. Available at: http://www.education.auckland.ac.nz/uoa/education/staff/j.hattie/presentations.cfm
20 Dinham, S. (2007). The lesson of Jonah. *Education Review, 17*(8), 5.

21 Dinham, S., Ingvarson, L., & Kleinhenz, E. (2008). Investing in teacher quality: Doing what matters most. In *Teaching talent: The best teachers for Australia's classrooms*. Melbourne: Business Council of Australia.
22 Dinham, S. (2006). Teaching and teacher education: Some observations, reflections and possible solutions. *ED Ventures*, 2, 3–20.
23 Dinham, Ingvarson, & Kleinhenz. (2008), p. 10.
24 McGaw, B. (2007). Crisis? The real challenges for Australian education. *Independent Education*, 37(2), 21–23.
25 See Scott, C. (2008). No gift for the talented: A lousy label for any child. *Professional Educator*, 7(1), 4–5.
26 Hattie, J. (2007).
27 Flynn, J. R. (1984). The mean IQ of Americans: Massive gains 1932 to 1978. *Psychological Bulletin*, 95, 29–51.
28 Neisser, U. (1997). Rising scores on intelligence test. *American Scientist*, 85, 440–447.
29 Dinham, S. (2007). How schools get moving and keep improving: Leadership for teacher learning, student success and school renewal. *Australian Journal of Education*, 51(3), 263–275.
30 Dinham, S. (2007). The waves of leadership. *The Australian Educational Leader*, 29(3), 20–21, 27.
31 Bransford, Brown, & Cocking, R. (2000); Donovan, M., Bransford, J., & Pellegrino, J. (Eds.). (1999). *How people learn: Bridging research and practice*. Washington, DC: National Academy Press.
32 Bransford, Brown, & Cocking (2000), pp. 14–27.

2 | Quality teaching in action

How can we know the dancer from the dance?
(W.B. Yeats, 'Among School Children')

Introduction

We have seen how two major factors influence student achievement: the quality of the teacher and the quality of teaching. In this chapter, we will examine the findings from a study of successful or quality teaching in an attempt to 'know the dancer (the teacher) from the dance (teaching)'. On the surface, both would seem to be closely intertwined.

One of my intended outcomes is for you to reflect on and relate the findings reported here to the research literature on quality teaching introduced in Chapter 1. An additional task is to relate these findings to your own teaching experience and your current context.

While the case study in this chapter is drawn from secondary teaching in one state and system, don't be put off by this if you work in another area of education. As noted below, responses to this work from primary and other non-secondary educators have been very positive because at the end of the day, good teaching is good teaching.[1]

Background to the NSW HSC study

This study of successful senior secondary teaching occurred in the late 1990s in government (public) schools in New South Wales, Australia. As noted previously, the Higher School Certificate (HSC) is a high-stakes credential that was first awarded in 1967. Although it has changed over the years in terms of how student performance in Years 11 and 12 is measured and reported, since that time it has remained the prime mechanism for measuring overall secondary achievement and allocating students to places in courses at NSW and other universities. Rather than being an overall 'mark' as it once was, the HSC today is a ranking exercise based on a combination of performance on in-school assessments and external examinations. By common consensus, the HSC has high credibility and acceptance worldwide as a rigorous credential.

In the minds of students, parents, the media and the community, great importance is placed upon the 'score' (actually a percentile ranking) that HSC students achieve. Schools are judged, and some choose to promote themselves, on the basis of the performance of their students at the HSC. University entry scores also contribute to the status of courses, faculties and universities as a whole. For example, in Australian universities medicine is typically the course with the highest entry requirement at those universities offering medical training, closely followed by law. Entry scores above the 99.5th percentile are usually required for entry to medicine, (although medical training in Australia is increasingly moving to graduate rather than school entry, i.e. students complete an undergraduate degree in a relevant area before entering medical training, something which is also occurring at some Australian universities with teacher education). Overall, the higher status, older universities (the 'sandstones' as they are termed) tend to have greatest demand for their courses and therefore the highest entry standards.

Entry standards to teacher education courses are also higher at the older, higher status universities, with scores above the 80th percentile common for 'straight' undergraduate education degrees, and above the 90th percentile for some double or joint degrees which are increasingly popular. At the regional universities, however, entry to primary teaching courses can be as low as the 60th percentile and even lower for students taking advantage of the various regional 'bonus' or 'principal recommendation' schemes. Entry to teacher education courses across Australia has generally declined since around 2005.[2]

The release of HSC results has become an annual ritual in NSW, with media reports on the 'best' students and attempts to formulate 'league tables' for school performance, often using crude indicators. Because of the intense interest the HSC increasingly engenders (which some would describe as a 'frenzy'), the body responsible for public education in NSW, the Department of Education and Training (NSW DET), commissioned a study from staff at the University of Western Sydney (UWS) to investigate teaching strategies leading to student success at the HSC. This chapter draws heavily on that study, which was completed in 1999 and released in 2000.

NSW HSC study

The study was conducted by Paul Ayres, formerly UWS and now at the University of NSW, Wayne Sawyer (UWS) and myself, formerly UWS and now with ACER. All three of us had been experienced HSC teachers in different subject areas.

The aims of the study were to:

- identify the relationship between teaching methods and HSC outcomes for students
- identify the characteristics of successful HSC teaching methodology
- consider the implications of the study findings for improving teacher efficiency.[3]

The budget for the study was modest, which limited its scope, but we were surprised by the interest it created. Copies of the 16-page summary of our report to the NSW DET[4] were sent to every secondary school in the state (nearly 400 high schools and almost 70 combined primary–secondary 'central' schools). As a result of demand, this summary was reprinted a number of times, not to mention photocopied and scanned unknown numbers of times, and a general version for Australia was later published.[5] This too created strong interest, and later a paper on the study was published internationally.[6] There were a variety of other publications and the three of us have been kept busy in the period since the release of the study giving presentations – which now probably run into the hundreds for the three of us combined – on the study's findings.

While we were pleased with the outcomes of study, as was the NSW DET, we were also initially puzzled by the strong enthusiasm for it, which came not just from those involved with senior secondary education and not just from public schools in NSW. Looking back, the study had struck a chord with teachers because it was about teaching and learning, and because the findings and examples came from real teachers and schools with which teachers could identify.

Faculties and school teams worked through the study summary and used it (and continue to do so, according to anecdotal feedback) as a framework for judging and improving their own effectiveness. It was frequently described to us as 'timely', not just because of the fixation with the HSC, but because schools then were in the midst of the 'managerial paradigm', with teaching and learning having low priority as leaders put their energies towards developing self-managing schools and engaging in school promotion and marketing. On many occasions I have been told by teachers that 'this is the most useful document to come out of the Department', no doubt an exaggeration but good recognition nevertheless.

The study report seemed to mark a return to core business in schools at a time when quality teaching was moving firmly onto the international agenda as evidenced by the release of some key OECD reports.[7]

Method

In designing the study, we were guided by the finding from the literature that experts often find it difficult to articulate what they do, something which tended to rule out some form of survey to ask teachers about their practices. We decided very early on that we needed to do several things: identify some highly successful senior secondary teachers, observe them teach, and talk to them and others about their teaching. This would be costly and would limit the number of teachers we could include in the study.

We were given access to confidential HSC performance data for government schools for the period 1991–96. Teachers were selected by first identifying a number of faculties (subject departments) that had demonstrated significant success at the HSC in certain subjects over a period of time (at least five years). Success was defined as having students in the top 1 per cent of the candidates for HSC courses (subjects often have several levels of difficulty and we looked at all courses, including lower level/ability courses).

We then used a variety of statistical 'filters' to eliminate variables other than the teacher as the cause for this success. We did this as follows: by comparing results achieved by other teachers with the same students at the same school; external comparisons within a course, especially for courses like languages with small numbers sitting the HSC; additional controls for academic selectivity (some secondary schools in NSW are academically selective with potential students undertaking a competitive examination at the end of Year 6 – these schools would be expected to achieve high results) and socio-economic status through comparing 'like with like' schools; observing the clustering of results over the time period, and considering who was teaching these classes in different years.

Thus, it was performance within a school by a teacher, as well as absolute performance in terms of state-wide HSC results that determined possible inclusion in the study.

Because of budgetary limitations and the desire to cover as best we could both the range of subjects and the types of secondary schools across the state, we finally settled on teachers in subject departments in 32 schools – 18 metropolitan (Sydney) and 14 non-metropolitan (regional urban and country). Of the 32 subject departments, seven were in academically selective high schools and 25 in comprehensive high schools. Because of the method used to select teachers and the need to cover the major subject areas* and broad socio-economic variety of the state in a representative

---

* Twelve subjects were represented in the study: Ancient History, Biology, Business Studies, English, Legal Studies, Mathematics, Modern History, Music, Personal Development Health and Physical Education (PDHPE), Physics, Society and Culture, Visual Arts.

fashion, we did not claim that the teachers chosen were the 'best' HSC teachers in NSW, merely that they appeared to be highly successful according to the criteria and data at our disposal. As will be seen, we feel we could have chosen another equally successful group of teachers had we had the time and money to do so.

Due to various constraints, we were able to visit only 17 of the 32 schools. In total, 25 teachers took part in the study where the typical methodology was to observe each teacher for two lessons or more, usually teaching Year 11 classes, and then interview the teachers both about the lesson observed and more generally about their teaching and professional development. We also sat in staff rooms and spoke to other teachers, head teachers (heads of department; eight study teachers were HoDs) and in some cases, students. Of the teachers participating in the study, 68 per cent were women, mirroring the sex distribution of women and men in secondary teaching in NSW, and most were very experienced, with an average of 17 years in their present school.

We had a number of concerns about the method we employed. The first was that the teachers we identified might not have been 'good' teachers at all, but 'rote learners', textbook teachers, and 'exam crammers' who 'taught to the test'. This was not the case with any of the teachers we observed. The second concern was that these teachers might have been talented isolates, 'high fliers' or 'lone rangers', not well integrated into their faculties or schools. Once again, our research findings proved otherwise. The third concern was that because of the limited time available, we would not be able to get an accurate view of their teaching – they would 'put on a show' for our benefit. This too was unfounded.

In the early stages, all three of us observed lessons until we were satisfied that the method and protocols (lesson observation schedules, interview questions, other structured and unstructured observations) were working successfully. After this pilot phase, usually only one of us was in the room. Even when all three were observing classes, it was obvious that once we were introduced to or observed by the class (the real reason for our presence was not provided to the students), the class and teacher quickly got down to work and we were ignored. Some teachers appeared nervous, but this soon vanished once the lesson started. In fact, we found that it was a feature of many of these teachers' teaching that other teachers were frequently in the room for various purposes – students were used to teachers dropping in and out.

A final point to add is that we genuinely enjoyed the research process. In this and other studies in which I have had the opportunity to watch expert teachers at work, it is always illuminating and sometimes inspiring. As an experienced teacher, I always see something that makes me reflect on my own teaching as well as learn more about teaching generally and there is something special about watching someone who is a master of their profession in action.

Factors contributing to senior secondary teaching success

We analysed our data using accepted content analysis techniques utilising spread sheets to record the frequency of various observation and interview phenomena.[8] As a result of this process, seven broad factors were identified as contributing to HSC teaching success. The essential features of each will be described:

- School background
- Subject faculty (department)
- Teachers' personal qualities
- Teachers' relationships with students
- Teachers' professional development
- Teaching – resources, planning
- Teaching strategies

1   School background

When we spoke to the selected teachers and their colleagues, there was a marked tendency to talk of the students at the school positively, regardless of how the school might have been regarded in the wider community. Terms used to describe students included 'motivated', 'friendly', 'disciplined', 'focused on learning' and just 'good kids'. A general finding drawn from this and other studies (see Chapter 3) is that positive attitudes are both indicative of a healthy school culture and contagious, in that they set up something of a self-fulfilling prophecy or upward cycle. Unfortunately, experience has shown that the reverse is also true. Students and schools can be talked down more easily than they can be talked up. Attitudes, expectations and mind-sets are powerful influences in schools, for good or bad.

Consistent with the positive way that students were regarded and described, the teachers in the faculties (once again, not just those selected for study) described their fellow teachers as 'supportive', 'hard-working' and 'caring'. They also commented on how school leaders provided support for their subject or faculty. Some spoke of the support of the community for their subject area.

Faculty members also commented on whole or cross-school approaches to curriculum and pedagogy, which they saw as contributing to student success at the HSC.

In the light of research findings about factors leading to student achievement identified by writers such as Hattie and Marzano in Chapter 1, school-based factors were reported by those involved with the HSC study to be influential, but of minor importance overall in the success of individual teachers and students. In other words, helpful, but not essential conditions for student success.

2   Subject faculty

As noted, we had wondered whether the teachers we selected for the study might have been misfits or loners. However, the message we got very quickly was how important subject departments or faculties were to the success of these individual teachers. In fact, a number of study teachers and other faculty members told us that while we had identified one teacher as being successful, there were others who were equally effective in the faculty and in the school generally. This was not said in any sense of criticism, professional jealousy or complaint but rather as free recognition of others' professional capacity.

Ways in which the faculty as a team influenced the success of individual teachers and their students included:

- *The faculty acting as a team:* This was demonstrated through sharing programs, resources and teaching ideas.
- *Faculty members setting the climate for all individuals within the faculty:* This could be summed up as 'we are professional, we have high expectations, we will help you as much as possible, but we expect you to play your part, meet our standards and support us in what we are trying to achieve'.
- *Whole-faculty approaches to programming:* With staff sharing responsibility for curriculum development.
- *The faculty having achieved a certain profile and identity within the school:* This led to comments like 'The teachers in the Science Faculty are up to date, innovative, hard-working and successful', and so forth.
- *Faculty success breeding success:* This was one of those 'ah ha' moments that sometimes occur with research. When we asked faculty members and those teachers selected for the study why they thought they were successful at the HSC, a majority stated independently that they laid the groundwork for HSC success by attracting talented junior students into the subject in Years 11–12 through their teaching in Years 7–10; 'setting up' students for HSC success through thorough teaching of fundamental knowledge and skills in Years 7–10, and through the subject having gained the status of a 'dominant culture' within the school, so that undertaking the subject was a sign of aspiration and ambition on the part of students, who expected to 'work hard and do well'.

- *Whole-faculty rapport with students:* As part of a strong and distinct faculty ethos and culture, general rapport with students was observed in classrooms, faculty staff rooms and in the school generally. There was obvious mutual respect and even affection between staff and students. One key observation was how staff members were prepared to assist the students of their fellow faculty members. One situation I observed is illustrative of this. I was sitting in a staff room used by visual arts teachers when a student knocked at the door. The student spoke briefly to her class teacher, asking for some assistance. The teacher listened carefully before saying something along the lines of 'You really need to speak to Ms ___ – she's the expert on that', at which point Ms ___ stopped what she was doing and went to the student's assistance. This phenomenon was repeated elsewhere in the study and indicates a number of things: these teachers were willing to speak with students during their breaks, which is not always the case; teachers were prepared to admit they didn't know everything – again, not universal amongst teachers; these teachers were comfortable about deferring to the superior knowledge of a colleague, and finally that a teacher was willing to help someone who wasn't their student. After observing this phenomenon a number of times, we came to the conclusion that this practice was analogous to a medical professional referring a patient to a specialist colleague.

There were other faculty features identified by teachers as being influential in their students' HSC success:

- The faculty was well organised with easy access to resources.
- The faculty had a general sense of enthusiasm and vitality.
- Faculty members 'loved' their subject and saw it as important to students.
- Faculties were very experienced.
- Faculty members were well prepared and up to date.
- The faculty aimed to give their subject(s) a high profile within the school.
- The faculty sometimes focused on specific purposes appropriate to the particular needs of students.

Once again, in line with other research literature, faculty-based factors were confirmed to influence teacher effectiveness and student achievement, more so than general school factors, although the influence was still less than that of the individual teacher, which is the direction in which this discussion now turns.

3 Teachers' personal qualities

Teachers' personal qualities (i.e. the dancer) emerged as an important factor in this research project. Key aspects are detailed below although there is understandable overlap with the factor of 'Teachers' relationships with students', which follows.

- *Orientation to subject:* the individual teacher's mastery of content knowledge and their belief that this was a key factor in their success was one of the key findings of the study. Strong subject content knowledge was evident in the lessons observed across the curriculum: 'You've got to know your stuff' was the most common response from teachers to questions about HSC success. This was also a strong factor influencing student confidence in the teacher and student success at the HSC. Teachers' love and passion for their subject was important in motivating students. In another one of those 'ah ha' moments, teacher after teacher told us that their particular subject (English, Maths, Legal Studies, or whatever) was the most important subject students undertook, the reason being that it was essential and would prepare them for life. This belief gave weight to their teaching, and teachers were constantly communicating to their students and reinforcing their belief in the importance and relevance of their subject.
- *Orientation to students:* approachability in and out of class was the important trait most readily identified here by these teachers. The teachers demonstrated a willingness to relax and to be themselves with students and were regarded by students as real people, and not remote, unapproachable authority figures (see below).
- *Orientation to work:* teachers described themselves and were described by others as 'hard-working' and 'committed'. Good organisation on the part of the teacher was seen as a key factor contributing to student confidence and success.

4   Teachers' relationships with students

Strong positive relationships with students formed an important background against which effective teaching occurred. Positive teacher–student relationships and effective teaching are mutually reinforcing, and in this case it was hard to discern cause and effect with each being in evidence.

Aspects of positive relationships with students exhibited by the teachers included:

- *Being themselves:* teachers' willingness and capacity to relax in the classroom, and not to appear remote, yet still to be unmistakably in control.
- *Relating to students as people:* it was apparent that the teachers had established appropriate personal and professional 'distance' with their students. Teachers took a personal interest in things such as sport, music and other student accomplishments through conversations in the playground and classroom, without prying too deeply or giving away too much personal information about themselves.
- *Mutual respect and discipline:* classes were calm and orderly and had a sense of purpose, with students interacting informally within unspoken yet

agreed limits. We saw no instance where a teacher needed to discipline a student. There was a jointly held expectation concerning what was acceptable behaviour. Students appeared to feel that they were respected for being 'seniors' and responded accordingly.
- *Teacher availability and approachability:* teachers were prepared and happy to take questions, help students and see them out of class time. Students saw teachers as being there to help if needed. They were not afraid to ask for assistance and didn't fear being ridiculed for asking a 'dumb question'.

5 Teachers' professional development

These teachers had achieved a certain profile, credibility and reputation within and outside their schools. Their expertise was recognised and sometimes sought out by others. Some had taken the lead in providing professional development within their school and through their involvement with professional associations outside the school.

A number of teachers mentioned how teachers from other schools would sometimes contact them to request copies of their teaching programs because of their HSC success, usually some time after the HSC results were released, but that these approaches were usually rebuffed. Aside from a reluctance to hand over their work to others, there was a view expressed that 'It's not just the program ... but what you do with it', to use the words of one teacher in the study.

- *Networking:* most of these teachers were active networkers which assisted both their professional learning and the learning of others. This occurred through membership of various groups, associations and committees. An interesting finding of the study was the high degree to which teachers were involved in professional practice in their 'host discipline'. For example, visual arts teachers were artists, music teachers were musicians, legal studies teachers were involved with the legal profession, science teachers were amateur astronomers, and so forth. These connections were beneficial in keeping these teachers in touch with developments in their field and added richness and relevance to their teaching.
- *In-school professional development:* about half the teachers saw their professional development as being based largely within their faculty. When teachers had been involved in in-service learning off-site, there was usually some form of demonstration or reporting back to fellow staff. Sometimes a head teacher or another mentor was cited by teachers as an important source of professional learning. Where teachers were in small faculties or were the only teacher of a subject in the school (as was the case with teachers of music and biology in the study), professional development, mentors and networks were often external to the school. Larger faculties were more self-contained when it came to professional learning.

- *Development through experience:* almost all of the teachers spoke of their accumulated experience as being important in their success, although they also recognised that experience or time alone was not sufficient to guarantee effectiveness. 'Rich' experience, professional learning and help from others were seen as necessary for development as an effective teacher, over and above time in the job.
- *Out-of-school professional development:* for those teachers who nominated out of school activities as the major source of their professional learning (around half of those studied), formal courses which provided 'subject content' were seen as most valuable by two-thirds of these teachers, while the remaining third cited courses about 'pedagogic content' or teaching strategies as being most valuable. While most of the teachers in the study took advantage of regular in-service, some teachers sought out particular courses to enrich their teaching; for example, one Ancient History teacher undertook a university course on hieroglyphics in her own time, other teachers planned their holidays to visit sites they would be teaching about.

6 Resources and planning

- *Planning:* over half the teachers identified planning as a key aspect of their success, both in terms of content and strategies, although content planning – what to teach – was more common.
- *Resources:* teachers were highly critical and selective users of resources and many had developed their own materials for teaching in collaboration with colleagues. Textbooks alone were seen as inadequate, both because these did not contain topical material and because they were not considered sufficiently challenging or innovative.

7 Teaching strategies

The identification of teaching strategies leading to HSC success was the central aim of the study. While it was possible to identify particular strategies and approaches that were more prominent in certain subject areas such as English,[9] overall, these successful teachers had far more in common than not.

Male and female teachers also had much in common in terms of both personal qualities and teaching strategies. There were no discernible 'male' or 'female' teaching styles.

What does come through from the study findings, was that these people were not born teachers. They did, however, have a passion for their subject and an enthusiasm to pass on to students what they know and 'love' about it. Overall, they possessed both deep content knowledge and strong pedagogic content knowledge – they knew what to teach and how to teach it. They also had an expert's understanding of the HSC process.

What follows is a description of teaching strategies employed by the teachers. As suggested by the literature, these teachers were not able to recall or describe fully the strategies they employed in the lessons that were observed.[10] Like experts in other fields and teachers in other studies, their actions and interventions frequently appeared to be arational and characterised by automaticity. However, like other experts, they saw more detail in their classrooms than would novice teachers, and were thus able to provide an appropriate intervention or variation in technique almost unthinkingly and instantaneously.[11]

In the discussion of teaching strategies that follows, there is inevitably some overlap with the previous sections; that is, the dancer with the dance.

a   Classroom climate

Aspects of classroom climate observed in these teachers' classes included:

- An unspoken expectation for students to demonstrate 'on task' behaviour existed, yet acceptable 'off-task' behaviour was tolerated.
- The rate of progress in lessons was often rapid, yet students were able to cope.
- In class, 'face-to-face' time was seen as precious, and not to be wasted, rather than having students' work mainly out of class or at home.
- Community or group learning was more common than expected.
- Teachers had enthusiasm and energy.
- Teachers reinforced students; gave feedback; recognised students' work and achievements.
- Regular routine and some repetition was seen as important in providing structure and order.
- Teachers showed interest in students' lives, as well as individual progress, allowing some informal time in class.
- An ethos of student co-operation and sharing in the classroom was developed, despite supposed competitive aspects of the HSC.

b   HSC focus

- Lessons were classed as 'HSC dominated' in half the lessons observed, in that the HSC was referred to or its requirements were addressed specifically.
- Half the teachers felt regular practice on specific HSC exam components was important; and provided 'tips' and strategies to tackle the course and exam.
- On the whole, the HSC was seen as a common goal, with rituals and rules that had to be met and faced; the teacher and students were on the 'same side'.
- Teachers went 'beyond' the HSC in many instances, 'teaching for understanding' rather than to pass an exam.

- Half the teachers felt their HSC marking experience was vital to their success (i.e. knowing marking standards, what markers looked for – most non-metropolitan teachers lacked this experience because of lack of opportunity to perform HSC marking, an equity issue for these teachers and their students, marking the HSC being commonly described by those who had the opportunity as 'great PD').
- Teachers were not 'exam crammers'.

c   Building understanding
- *The interrelatedness of the subject:* teachers continually linked different areas and topics of the subject, previous lessons, to develop a 'big picture'; the emphasis was on finding multiple solutions rather than advocating or practising one 'best way'; use of previous knowledge to find these solutions.
- *Using students' responses:* students' responses were used as building blocks, with the teacher drawing out responses without providing answers.
- *Facilitating thinking through applying knowledge and solving problems:* the emphasis was on applying knowledge in class time, using reasoning, independent thinking and group work.
- *Interpretation:* emphasis was on interpretation, rather than reproduction of knowledge.
- *DARTS (Direct Activities Related to Texts):*[12] e.g. cloze, prediction, categorising, labelling and sequencing exercises were used.
- *Games, simulations and stories:* e.g. scenarios, role-plays, songs, setting up a business.

d   Note-making
- *Building notes:* through teacher facilitation; recording student discussion, directed note-making and student summaries; from student research, from student presentations; filling in gaps in knowledge.
- *Independent note-making:* little class time devoted to 'note-taking' and notes rarely distributed; independent 'note-making' and thinking encouraged, e.g. by having students complete notes from research/discussion, directed note-making (see above), student note-sharing from seminars or group work, allowing students latitude to decide what to record depending on individual need, reviewing class work in the student's 'own words', making own notes which the teacher checked – all leading to student 'ownership' of notes and obviating need for further note-making and summaries out of class time.

e   Writing essays and organising information
- *'Big' essays or projects often seen as worthless:* emphasis instead was on writing within the time scale of the HSC exam (i.e. write 250 words in 10

minutes); work on essay technique; provision of positive essay examples (e.g. 'this paper is worth 18/20 because …').
- *Answering problems:* importance of 'stretching', 'challenging' students, and not 'talking down to', or 'leading students by the hand' was recognised; teachers refused to provide 'ready-made' solutions to problems; students were encouraged to find solutions using the foundation provided by teacher.

f Questioning

Some of us may have been told that *closed questions* are 'bad' (only one answer; 'guess what's in the teacher's head'; stifles discussion) and *open questions* are 'good' (a number of possible answers, interpretations; promotes discussion and thinking).[13]

However, when the lesson observations were coded, there were many examples of closed questions, along with many open questions, which seemed to contradict the view about the importance of teachers emphasising reasoning, understanding, thinking and interpretation through the use of open questions.

After analysis and reflection, the key to this apparent contradiction was discovered. These teachers used different forms of questioning depending on the stage of the lesson and whether the teacher was teaching the whole class or if students were working alone or in small groups.

Teachers tended to use closed questions when talking to the whole group and at the beginning and end of lessons to link, revise and test understanding. This also occurred at certain break points in lessons when students were passing from one activity to the next.

Open questions tended to be used when teachers wanted students to explore, interpret, predict or explain individually or in small groups. No teacher was able to tell us that they were using this approach, but virtually all did, and it makes perfect sense in hindsight.

- *Whole-class questioning:* closed questions dominated whole-class discussion (assessment, review, linking, building), yet open questions were used for individuals and groups to promote deeper thinking.

g Whole-class discussion, group work and independent student activity

- *Discussion:* a climate of open debate was encouraged, with presentation of different views, respect for all opinions, 'filtered' through teacher.
- *Group work:* small groups were used in one-third of observed lessons; two-thirds of teachers said they used this technique; groups were used for making deductions from source material, learning from each other, finding out for themselves, solving problems; teachers used this time for

one-to-one assistance of students, prompting, challenging and providing individual feedback.
- *Independent student activity:* these included presentations of seminars by students, peer teaching, individual out-of-class research.

h Assessment

Two things that characterised the teaching of these successful teachers were frequent, varied assessment, and frequent, constructive feedback designed to help students to understand what they can and can't do, and what they need to do in order to do better.[14] Assessment and feedback each took a variety of forms, both informal and formal.
- *Techniques:* short tests, quizzes, instant feedback for teacher and students; student work marked while students worked; sometimes the whole lesson was used for evaluation; providing a lot of feedback seen as important; monitoring of every student's progress.

i Other strategies

A variety of other strategies were observed or reported by teachers.
- question/answer/explain; pattern of demonstration/application, portion of lesson as lecture; concrete aids to recall (mind-maps, time-lines, colours, graphs, songs); having students use imagination (visualisation, drawing parallels with today, imagining, role-playing); students using board to demonstrate; taking students to lectures, extra-curricular activities (e.g. mock trials), using real-world examples.

Conclusion to discussion of the senior secondary successful teaching study

The study identified senior secondary teachers who were successful over a period of five years in getting some of their students in the top 1 per cent of the state. We had been concerned that these teachers might have been exam 'crammers' who 'taught to the test', and that their teaching may have only been suited to the more 'academic' students in their classes. However, the study revealed that not only were these teachers successful with the top students but that they had also lifted the performance of most of their students relative to these students' performance in other subjects.

To sum up, these teachers were genuinely expert in their subject area(s), and clearly enjoyed teaching. Although a wide range of teaching strategies was observed, the key common factor was an emphasis on having students think, solve problems and apply knowledge. These teachers consciously built understanding and connected students' work to previous work, work that was yet to come, and events in the broader environment. Frequent assessment and quality feedback were hallmarks of these teachers. Rather than teaching *to* the HSC, these teachers saw their role as challenging students *beyond* the demands of the HSC.

Mutual respect, confidence and high expectations were features of classroom lessons. Good relationships and positive classroom climate were also universally observed.

Assisted note-building, ownership of note-making and economic use of class time were other features of the teaching observed. Despite the competitive nature of the HSC, the use of group work was more common than might have been expected.

While the HSC was a constant presence in the classrooms of these teachers, what was seen was broadly consistent with our understanding of quality teaching from other research. Consistent with the literature, quality teaching was found to be the major factor in the success of these students, although other faculty and school factors were important.

Personal qualities, experience, deep content knowledge, strong pedagogic knowledge, understanding of the HSC and its requirements, and use of appropriate and effective teaching strategies all led to teacher effectiveness and student achievement. Again, these findings are consistent with the broader literatures on student achievement and effective or quality teaching.

We will now consider in detail how leadership can be exercised to create a situation in which teacher learning, quality teaching and student success can occur.

Acknowledgements

The permission of Paul Ayres and Wayne Sawyer to reproduce material from our publications arising from the HSC study is gratefully acknowledged.

Notes
1. See Dinham, S. (2002). NSW Quality Teaching Awards – Research, rigour and transparency, *Unicorn, 28*(1), 5–9.
2. Dinham, S., Ingvarson, L., & Kleinhenz, E. (2008). Investing in teacher quality: Doing what matters most. In *Teaching talent: The best teachers for Australia's classrooms*. Melbourne: Business Council of Australia.
3. Ayres, P., Dinham, S., & Sawyer, W. (1999). *Successful teaching in the NSW Higher School Certificate*. Sydney: NSW Department of Education and Training.
4. Ayres, P., Dinham, S., & Sawyer, W. (1998). *The identification of successful teaching methodologies in the NSW Higher School Certificate. A Research Report for the NSW Department of Education and Training*. Penrith: University of Western Sydney, Nepean.

5 Ayres, P., Dinham, S., & Sawyer, W. (2000). Successful senior secondary teaching. *Quality Teaching Series*. No. 1, Australian College of Education, September, 1–20.
6 Ayres, P., Dinham, S., & Sawyer, W. (2004). Effective teaching in the context of a Grade 12 high stakes external examination in New South Wales, Australia. *British Educational Research Journal*, *30*(1), 141–165.
7 Organisation for Economic Co-operation and Development. (1994). *Quality in Teaching*. Paris: Author; Organisation for Economic Co-operation and Development. (2004). *Education at a glance: OECD Indicators 2004*. Paris: Author.
8 Ayres, P., Dinham, S., & Sawyer, W. (1997). *The identification of successful teaching methodologies in the NSW Higher School Certificate: Identifying the successful teachers*. Penrith: University of Western Sydney, Nepean.
9 Sawyer, W., Ayres, P., & Dinham, S. (2001). What does an effective Year 12 English teacher look like? *English in Australia*, *129*(30), 51–63.
10 Berliner, D. (2004). Describing the behaviour and documenting the accomplishments of expert teachers. *Bulletin of Science, Technology & Society*, *24*(3), 200–212.
11 Bransford, J., Brown, A., & Cocking, R. (Eds.). (2000). *How people learn* (pp. 31–50). Washington, DC: National Academy Press.
12 Lunzer, E., & Gardner, K. (1984). *Learning from the written word*. London: Oliver & Boyd.
13 See Barnes, D. Language in the secondary classroom. In Barnes, D., Britton, J., & Rosen, H. (1974). *Language, the learner and the school*. Harmondsworth: Penguin.
14 Dinham, S. (2008). Feedback on feedback. *Teacher*, May, 20–23.

3 What effective school leaders do to promote teaching and learning

All mankind is divided into three classes: those who are immovable, those who are movable; and those who move.

(Benjamin Franklin)

Introduction

We have seen how research has clearly demonstrated the important influence of the classroom teacher on student achievement, and what successful teaching looked like in one context.

As noted, the key challenge for educational leaders is to make things happen in individual classrooms, particularly given the well-known professional isolation of teachers and the equally well-known variation in teacher effectiveness.

This chapter explores how school leaders and teams acted to promote quality teaching and student achievement in 38 schools.

The study of senior secondary teaching discussed previously focused on successful individual teachers. An unexpected finding of that study was the degree to which the success of these teachers was found to be underpinned by faculties and teams.

AESOP (An Exceptional Schooling Outcomes Project) aimed to investigate junior secondary education – Years 7–10 – rather than senior secondary education. It was decided to investigate the junior secondary years because this stage of schooling has been relatively neglected and is something of a 'black hole'.

The junior secondary years represent a transition from the traditional model of primary school to secondary schooling, with its multiple teachers and discrete subjects. The junior secondary years also mark the period during which the physical, emotional and social development of young people intensifies. Alienation and disengagement from schooling can occur at this time, to the extent that some students leave (or are encouraged to leave) school once they pass the age for compulsory attendance. Achievement gaps already evident at the end of primary school can widen during the junior secondary years. One response to these perceived problems has been the so-called 'middle schooling movement'.[1]

Background to the AESOP study

AESOP was a far larger project than the HSC study which spawned it, and was funded by the Australian Research Council. The major research partners were again the New South Wales Department of Education and Training (NSW DET) and the University of Western Sydney (UWS), which were joined for this project by staff at the University of New England (UNE).

As noted, the project was designed to investigate processes leading to exceptional educational outcomes in Years 7–10 in NSW government (public) schools. Exceptional educational achievement was defined using the rubric of the three interrelated domains or principles outlined in *The Adelaide Declaration on National Goals for* [Australian] *Schooling in the Twenty-first Century*;[2] that is, schools should:

1   'develop fully the talents of all students'
2   attain 'high standards of knowledge, skills and understanding through a comprehensive and balanced curriculum'
3   be 'socially just'.

Thus, we were concerned with conceptualising student achievement in a more holistic sense, rather than focusing on academic results alone.

Originally our major focus was to be subject departments (faculties), but as a result of our discussions and our desire to utilise the framework of the Adelaide Goals, we decided to include teams responsible for cross- or whole-school programs.

Research sites were thus to be of two types: departments responsible for teaching certain subjects in Years 7–10 (which we decided would be around 80 per cent of sites), and teams responsible for cross-school programs in Years 7–10 (the remaining 20 per cent of sites).

How the case study sites were selected

Our budget and methodology meant we could study about 50 sites across the state. Selection of the sites where exceptional outcomes were thought to be occurring was time-consuming and complex. The project methodology employed a case study approach whereby quantitative data (e.g. public examination performance, various 'value-adding' measures of student achievement growth) and qualitative data (e.g. nomination from parent groups, principals, DET officers) were used to select a sample of sites where schools *appeared* to have been achieving exceptional educational outcomes, either within faculty-based subject areas or with cross-school programs, over at least four years.

Triangulation and analysis of quantitative and qualitative selection data occurred, with sites selected to provide a sample of socio-economic types, rural–urban distribution, size of school, and spread of subject areas and programs. As with the previous study, there was no claim that these sites were the 'best', but based upon our selection criteria, they could be considered to be among the best in the state on a range of measures, confirmation or otherwise of which would come later.

As noted, use of the Adelaide Goals played an important role in the selection process, in that evidence of 'personal' and 'social' achievement was sought in addition to academic success. Eventually, 50 sites were selected for study at 38 secondary schools, with some schools selected for (potentially) exceptional educational achievement in two or more areas.

Formulation of project methodology and selection of sites took much of 2001. Pilot studies at four sites took place in late 2001, with the bulk of site visits taking place in 2002 and 2003. Analysis and writing for this major project were still taking place in 2006. The findings for the project were released in 2007.

How AESOP data were obtained and analysed

The overall aim of the project was:

> To identify and analyse processes in NSW public schooling, Years 7 to 10, producing exceptional educational outcomes to assist national renewal in junior secondary education.*

The following study questions were developed in respect of the above aim:

1 What are the variables and processes leading to outstanding educational outcomes – in the possible areas of personal identity, academic success and social attainment in the study site(s)?
2 Is it possible to identify the relationship(s), if any, between 'academic success', 'personal identity' and 'social attainment' as achieved through subject departments and/or other formal groups and special programs and initiatives?

---

* See http://www.une.edu.au/simerr/pages/projects/aesop.php

3   What organisational and institutional factors – NSW DET, district, school, leadership, community, faculty, other groups and individuals – contribute to and constrain this success?
4   To what degree and through what means, if any, are the outstanding educational outcomes of the sites shared or shareable with others within and beyond the school?

Participation on the part of schools, teams, and individuals was voluntary. Site visit research teams consisted of a university academic who acted as site team leader, another academic with expertise in the area under investigation (e.g. a maths education specialist), a head teacher (faculty head) from another school in the District with expertise in the subject under investigation, and the Chief Education Officer (School Improvement) from the local DET District. Additional academics and head teachers were included in multi-site visits.

Having an academic lead the research teams was important, as we realised early on that some school staff had suspicions about the study, seeing it as a departmental school 'review' or inspection by stealth, rather than a university research project.

It is also worth noting that the head teachers who were part of the site case study teams universally described the experience as a career highlight and one of the 'best' professional development activities they had ever undertaken. They enjoyed the whole experience of visiting another school, observing lessons, speaking with staff, students and community members, examining resources, making observations of various sorts and being part of a research team and the recognition this entailed. A view commonly expressed was that they were going to go back to their schools motivated to make changes in the light of what they had seen in these sites and schools.

Site teams were expected to undertake the following in four days or more:

- interview the principal about the outstanding faculty/program
- interview the head teacher/leader of the outstanding faculty/program
- with classroom teacher approval, visit classes to observe students at work, and discuss pedagogy and related matters with those teachers
- hold a faculty forum (faculty/program staff meeting)
- conduct student focus discussions with two year groups – Years 7 and 8, and Years 9 and 10
- conduct a parent forum
- team leader to organise additional discussions with the principal and perhaps the head teacher as needed

- team to investigate any documents that are held and used by the faculty/program, e.g. policy documents, newsletters, management plans, programs, etc.
- provide verbal feedback to the faculty/program staff and principal on the last day of the visit.

Site teams observed, interviewed, investigated and discussed intensively over the week, using protocols to record data and observations. Most interviews and focus groups were audio-taped. In country areas, teams usually stayed at the same accommodation and discussions took place 'after hours' as members came to an understanding of what they were encountering.

Teams collaboratively completed a detailed report in electronic format, usually within a month of the site visit. These reports were not provided to schools for reasons of confidentiality and concerns over the use of report findings – a few schools had publicised the fact that they had been selected for the study as proof of their effectiveness and success – but principals and relevant staff were provided with a verbal briefing of the broad findings for their school on the final day of the visit, feedback they appeared to find useful.

As a result of the AESOP study, there was a range of conference presentations and symposia presented over the course of the study in Australia and overseas. The major outcome of the project, however, was a set of books provided to every public secondary school in NSW and made available for general sale. There were also additional publications in the leadership area.[3]

The publications below reflected the major foci of the study, although some small subject and program areas that were studied were not included in the series:

- *Exceptional outcomes in English education* – Wayne Sawyer, Paul Brock and David Baxter
- *Exceptional outcomes in ESL/Literacy education* – Wayne Sawyer, David Baxter and Paul Brock
- *Exceptional outcomes in Mathematics education* – John Pegg, Trevor Lynch and Debra Panizzon
- *Exceptional outcomes in Science education* – Debra Panizzon, Geoffrey Barnes and John Pegg
- *Exceptional educational equity programs* – Lorraine Graham, David Paterson and Robert Stevens
- *Exceptional student welfare programs* – David Paterson, Lorraine Graham and Robert Stevens
- *Leadership for exceptional educational outcomes* – Steve Dinham.[4]

Most of the above were based on reports from three to five sites, although in the case of leadership, this was based on reports from all 38 schools, as data regarding leadership were evident in every report.

How does leadership contribute to outstanding educational outcomes in junior secondary schooling?

Leadership, both positional (principals, deputy principals, other school executive staff, relevant head teachers) and distributed (key classroom teachers and others), was found in this study to be a major factor in the outstanding outcomes achieved by students, teachers and schools.

Once again, there were surprises in the findings. It was expected that head teachers (faculty heads) and whole-school program leaders would be important to the success of faculties and teams, and this was confirmed.[5] Unexpected was the extent to which principals were found to have influenced the achievements of these faculties and teams – there were no specific questions asked about the principal's role in facilitating student or faculty achievement in our protocols and data about leadership emerged inductively – leading to the hypothesis that the influence of leaders, and especially principals, on student achievement may have been underestimated, possibly because this influence is indirect and difficult to measure. Another way to look at this is that in many or most schools, the influence exerted by principals and other leaders on student achievement might be in line with the general literature, but that this influence has the potential to be far greater, with commensurate effects on teacher quality and student achievement. It could be that it was this latter phenomenon that was seen to be operating in the majority of the AESOP sites.

In light of the above, it should be noted that while the vast majority of the 50 sites (arguably 46 or more) were confirmed to be achieving exceptional educational outcomes as defined by the project, some were not. In the cases that weren't, some aspects of leadership identified in the exceptional sites were lacking to some degree or largely absent.

The discussion in this chapter mainly concentrates on principal leadership, although there were parallels across the various levels and types of leadership. Leadership by deputy principals, head teachers, other executive and teacher leadership is considered in more detail elsewhere.[6]

Approximately equal numbers of male and female principals were represented in the 38 schools. No differences between the leadership styles or attributes of men or women principals (or other leaders) were discerned, but as noted, there were qualitative differences between these principals, and others leading schools which were not performing as effectively, both in the AESOP study and in other studies with which I have been involved.

From analysis of data on principal leadership from the site reports (using the qualitative data analysis software NUD*IST[7] and grounded theory procedures[8]), a set of seven categories of principal leadership attributes and practices contributing to exceptional educational outcomes were developed. These are represented in Figure 3.1. Each is discussed below, with the core category 'Focus on students, learning and teaching' discussed last. Inevitably, there is some overlap between each of the broad categories, with each attribute or approach related to others through the actions of the principal.

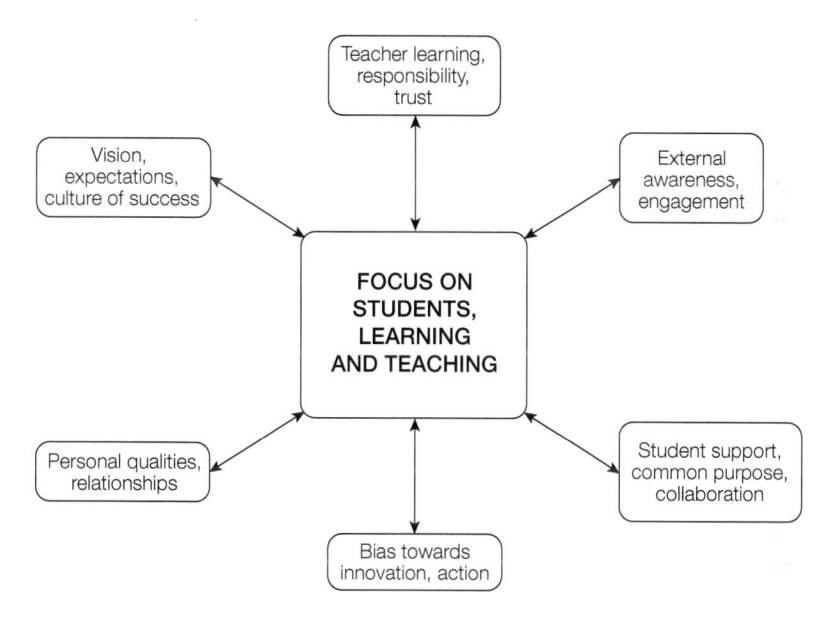

Figure 3.1 Principal leadership for exceptional student outcomes

1 External awareness and engagement

Principals of schools in which sites achieving exceptional outcomes were identified and confirmed exhibited a keen awareness and understanding of the wider environment and a positive attitude towards engaging with it.

At a time when so much is imposed on schools and many teachers and executive staff feel overwhelmed by change, defensive and disempowered,[9] it was apparent that principals in these schools possessed and demonstrated a positive attitude towards change. Rather than perceiving change as a threat, principals were open to the opportunities offered by change. Even with mandated change, principals looked for ways in which they could adapt and improve what they were already doing to meet new requirements, and considered ways in which their school might benefit from being in the forefront of change. As one site report* for a school identified for successful student welfare programs noted:

> *Even with mandated requirements, the Principal doesn't resort to line management, but draws out the positive aspects for the school of whatever is being required and 'sells' the change. What others would see as a problem, he sees as an opportunity. This positive mind-set is contagious. As the Principal noted: 'We do what we have to do, but we do it with gusto if we see that it helps'.*

Instead of attempting to keep change at bay, these principals exposed their school to the opportunities and challenges brought by change. Rather than being inward looking, they sought out, fostered, and utilised external networks and resources to assist with change. It was observed by a staff member that her school participated in 'every trial and pilot program' because of the benefits derived from being in the vanguard of change.

The external links principals sought to develop ranged from the local community through to the international level. These principals were found to be entrepreneurial in obtaining financial and in-kind support from the system, government, community and the corporate sector. They skilfully utilised such support and resources to realise their vision for the school. One site report for a school identified for ICT across the curriculum noted:

> *Personal networking [by the Principal] has been core to developing community perceptions of [the School] as a school displaying excellence in ICT across the curriculum. This has been fundamental in [the school] achieving and maintaining Apple Distinguished School status as well as opening up opportunities to trial DET ICT initiatives such as broadband communications.*

These leaders placed a high priority on establishing and maintaining good communications and relationships with external stakeholders. In schools with a high proportion of non-English speaking background parents and community members, emphasis was placed on communication through the use of interpreters, translators and community liaison officers. School signage and communications utilised the predominant languages of the community. Representatives of various disadvantaged groups spoke positively of the respect shown to them by the Principal and the school. They felt informed, valued and listened to, with the school open to them and their concerns.

---

* Site reports were completed collaboratively by the university and DET members of the case study teams.

As part of their open perspective, these principals were prepared to seek outside assistance when they couldn't solve problems. They were not afraid to 'put their hand up' for help and didn't see this as a sign of failure or inadequacy. A powerful example of this was detailed in the site report for one school. The Principal had earned considerable staff respect for his handling of a crisis in mid-2001 created by a small group of, in his words, 'angry, aggressive ... students' [of a certain cultural background]. At that time he was handling up to 20 'serious incident' reports each year and concluded:

> *When I reflected on it I thought that perhaps the way we were managing some of these situations was contributing to them. The other situation was that basically whenever there was a problem they looked for me or [the Deputy Principal] and sometimes that took five or ten minutes ... [The Principal took the issue to District Office] I put my hand up and said 'I'm going under!'. And I'll be honest with you, there are several elements to this. By the time I came here I had been a Principal for three years, but the enormity of this task was [too much] ... Dealing day-to-day with crises and nothing else took its toll and I was really afraid we were going to have a death. If it wasn't me it'd be someone else. By that stage I'd been spat on, chased ... I nearly had a brick through my head ... people were looking to me for leadership, and I honestly didn't have the answers. So, my response was to ... change our practices ... [but] It was bigger than I could handle. At that stage I thought I was on my own ... [but the District Office training program and assistance] has been able to facilitate my growth and the School's growth.*

Shortly after the training program there was a critical incident that invoked the processes adopted by the school 'for real'. With some satisfaction the Principal said:

> *People [now] know the language of how to deal with kids in certain situations. ... body language ... we no longer go in singly, we go in twos, we know how to separate fights, we know how to do a whole range of things. The feedback from my Executive is the best feedback that I've got, and that's something that has changed the culture of the school.*

Allied to openness to change and opportunity, these leaders have positive attitudes that tend to be contagious. They realise negativity can be self-handicapping ('misery loves company') and attempt to drive it out. Their positive approach motivates others and acts as a form of organisational energy to keep the school moving and improving. This is not blind, unthinking 'Pollyanna'-like optimism or 'always looking on the bright side of life', but is based on a realistic appraisal of the situation. Their positive approach is seen as authentic rather than a mechanism for manipulation or control. In the early 1950s Norman

Vincent Peale wrote an international bestseller *The power of positive thinking*. This power was clearly demonstrated in the site reports from the AESOP study.

2 A bias towards innovation and action

Three broad approaches were discerned in the actions of the principals of schools in which sites achieving exceptional outcomes were identified. These principals:

1. used their powers and the rules and boundaries of the 'system' creatively
2. exhibited a bias towards experimentation and risk taking
3. demonstrated strength, consistency, yet flexibility in decision making and the application of policy and procedures.

The schools tended to have a strong executive structure with clear, well-understood responsibilities. Rather than being dictatorial or autocratic, principals were seen to use these structures and responsibilities responsibly and effectively. They utilised the discretion available to them and pushed against administrative and systemic constraints when necessary. They creatively used resources at their disposal to support innovative programs and encouraged and supported staff to leave their 'comfort zones'. At times, they tended to be ahead of the system and profession and acted as 'ground-breakers'. They had earned a certain amount of credibility with system officials who tended to give special dispensation, support or approval to new approaches, even 'turning a blind eye' on occasion. Some even appeared to operate on the principle that 'it is easier to gain forgiveness than permission' from their superiors. (When I mention this point in conference presentations, principals smile and nod while system officials look apprehensive.)

In line with their outward-looking, positive nature, these principals were found to be informed risk takers. When an opportunity or problem arose, or even if things appeared to be going well, they were prepared to experiment and to offer support to those proposing initiatives. They were also prepared to risk time, money and failure, and empowered others to do the same. One principal commented: 'People are allowed to make mistakes here'. Staff at other schools made similar comments. These principals don't say 'yes' to every request, but they do use 'yes' to empower and recognise others. (Less effective principals were observed in this and other studies to use 'no' as a means of controlling staff.)

These principals don't dismiss a good idea because they didn't think of it, and they are not threatened by confident, talented staff. Their attitude can be summed up as 'Let's give it a go', although this decision is based on a rapid, full consideration of the issue under deliberation.

Site reports at three separate schools were illustrative of this approach:

> The Principal's leadership style is a critical precursor to the process being undertaken at [the school]. She is a risk taker and is prepared to 'work the system' to achieve her goals.

> Leadership at the school is outstanding. The Principal cultivates the trust of his staff by showing support for them to take risks and they return that trust by a willingness to improve processes that will benefit students. The Principal takes a strong role in selection of staff.

> The senior Executive of the school, and in particular the Principal, is held in high regard. The Principal is described [by staff] as a leader who provides subtle guidance and direction and allows people to try new ideas if they will improve students' learning.

Principals were found to have a major influence on the development and application of school policies and programs. Some leaders and staff characterised these as 'zero tolerance', but in reality this was more a case of having clear guidelines, effective communication and consistent application, with everyone knowing where he or she 'stands'. In this respect, the standard and routine things are done well. Students know what to do and who to seek help from when problems arise and often this understanding begins in primary 'feeder' schools with visits from key secondary staff and orientation visits to the secondary school playing an important role in easing the Year 6 to 7 primary–secondary transition.

However, this is not to imply rigidity, with principals and other leaders prepared to consider every case on its merits and to exercise discretion and compassion when needed. We saw and heard of many examples of such flexibility and compassion (see below). These leaders are able to sustain innovation in the face of increasing standardisation and accountability in education.

3 Personal qualities and relationships

Principals at the outstanding sites were found to possess and utilise high-level interpersonal skills and are liked and respected, often, but not always, by all. Their motives and actions are trusted by others. They use people's names when out and about in the school and show interest in what others are doing. They demonstrate empathy and compassion and are available at short notice when needed. They are seen to work for the school rather than for themselves and model 'do as I do', rather than 'do as I say'. They epitomise the notion of the 'servant leader', while being unmistakeably in control.

Students, staff and community members spoke positively of principals who were 'open', 'honest', 'fair', 'friendly' and 'approachable'. They valued the fact that the principal will 'listen' to them and hear what they say, thus showing respect. A head teacher (faculty head) at one school noted:

> [The Principal] has attracted creative people in the past five years. He is very supportive of staff, a great mentor. He creates a strong learning culture at the school. He knows the system and works well at District level ... He is highly visible in the school. Everyone feels they are special, and valued as people. He sets a very positive tone in the school.

A school counsellor (psychologist) at the same school commented:

> [The Principal] is one of the best I have worked with. Students know they can speak to him. He is highly approachable. He can speak in a nice tone to staff, parents and students. He is not authoritarian but he does set parameters. He is a good listener, supportive and encouraging. He will not contradict any proposal you present for his consideration but may suggest ideas to build on your proposal. He leads and guides rather than dictates.

A Year 11 student at another school spoke of the personal qualities of her Principal:

> The Principal is a nice guy. He talks to us. He even knows our name. You often see him out walking around in the playground. [The site report noted:] Parents, too, spoke about 'his open door policy' commenting that they felt comfortable phoning the Principal to discuss issues relating to their own children or the school.

A site report from another school noted:

> The school Principal has a genuine concern for the well-being of the students and an excellent rapport with both staff and students. He appears to make a considerable effort to get out of his office and has a high profile around the school.

These leaders were seen to possess and exhibit the characteristics they expect of others such as honesty, fairness, compassion, commitment, reliability, hard work, trustworthiness and professionalism. They provide a 'good example'. They also tend to have a social justice agenda, believing in education for social good and the importance of putting students first. A site report noted:

> The Principal creates a school culture in which recognition of differences is central. She sees herself as having a vocation of social justice that permeates much of the school. She believes in the dignity of humanity, has a sense of social justice and is able to translate this into effective action.

Another site report noted:

> *[The Principal] sets a very positive tone at the school. He is not a 'micro-manager', and gives staff 'space' and discretion to develop initiatives. He is seen as a person who can influence and role model rather than demand compliance. He is not defensive, not authoritarian and gives a measure of autonomy while overseeing effectively. He puts the focus on the enterprise, rather than on himself and ... models openness and self-evaluation. He cultivates a climate of trust. He places great trust in his staff and strongly supports them in any initiatives. The trust he places in his staff is returned, as indicated by a willingness to participate in process improvement and innovative problem solving.*

A research team at another school reported on what has been termed 'moral' or 'authentic' leadership:[10]

> *An important part of the success of this school, as with any school, is attributable to the role of the Principal. The Principal ... models quality interpersonal relationships and has an established presence and role in the management of student welfare programs. The professional and interpersonal dynamics which he nurtures and encourages in the faculties of the school leads to constant concern and productive dialogue about welfare and curriculum areas. During his interview the Principal articulated his drive to develop 'programs that are fair to kids'.*

Intellectual capacity is a factor frequently overlooked in discussions on successful leadership and quality teaching. These principals were generally seen to possess a high degree of intelligence and imagination. They are good judges of individuals, astute, and are able to balance 'big picture' issues with finer detail. They have good recall of the multitude of issues, facts and problems that make up the work of the principal and can pick up the threads of previous, often truncated conversations. They can deal with many issues concurrently and know when to consult and to build consensus and when to be decisive and to act alone. They understand school, departmental and community 'politics' and have the courage to make unpopular decisions when these are in the best interests of the school.

They are good communicators and listeners and provide prompt feedback and appropriate recognition to staff. Their support for staff was frequently noted in site visit reports. They make themselves available and are prepared to 'drop everything' and 'roll their sleeves up' to assist when and where necessary. In this way, they 'lead from the front'. We were told of instances where crises had occurred (sudden death of staff or students, violent incidents, tragedies of various sorts) where the principal had stepped into a difficult situation to take control and had supported staff and students.

4 Vision, expectations and a culture of success

These principals did not attempt to 'build Rome in a day'. They recognised the imperative for change and improvement but also realised that overburdened and at times dispirited staff cannot be given more than they can reasonably be expected to handle. However, this does not preclude them from being decisive when necessary.

Recognition of context is important, but it's also important not to be so bound up in context that one fails either to see the wider environment or to act. Context can be like quicksand. These leaders managed to have a broader perspective, yet recognised and addressed local context.

These leaders also possessed a long-term vision and agenda and were prepared to work towards this. Put simply, I like to define vision as 'knowing where you are going'. There is no point in trying to stand still or to keep change at bay as the world will pass you by and the organisation will be disadvantaged.

These principals set meaningful, achievable goals rather than short-term targets. The norm for principals was six to seven years in their current school, and when they had not been in their position for this length of time, had often served in the same school as a deputy principal or faculty head, helping them to get to 'know the territory'. An implication is that 'quick fixes' or 'flurries of change'[11] are unlikely to be successful. It takes time to break existing patterns of thought, behaviour and practice and to achieve effective and lasting change. In a number of sites, the school had been in decline prior to the appointment of the principal, suffering a fall in reputation and losing students, staff and resources. It had taken time and much effort, but things have 'turned around' such that some of these schools were now full to capacity with the principal having to deal with the politics of not being able to accommodate all requests for enrolment.

These leaders identified and nurtured the 'seeds' for change and school improvement. They recognised and valued the history of the school and use what has been achieved or what exists as a platform for further school improvement, thereby, releasing latent 'organisational energy'. The site report for one school identified for ICT, which had previously been in decline but was now 'bursting at the seams' with students, noted:

> *The current educational outcomes have their antecedents in the appointment of the current Principal in 1996. Staff universally point to her leadership, as well as the influence of others, on the school achieving outstanding educational outcomes since her appointment ... Clearly, the process is being driven from the top. The Principal has championed the infusion of ICT since her arrival ... She is aware of the potential of ICT as a tool for learning and discovery.*

An aspect of the vision demonstrated by principals was the ability to see the 'big picture' and to communicate this to staff. A site team noted:

> The Principal's leadership provides key input on critical issues, supports the positive culture of the school and helps to establish 'big picture issues' as priorities. Under the current Principal, [the school] has a commitment to student welfare, with an emphasis on continual improvement and ensuring quality communication with parents.

One way this vision is communicated and becomes reality is through the expectations of the principal. It was found that these leaders have high and clearly understood expectations of others (and importantly, themselves) and do not easily accept 'second best'. As noted by one member of staff: 'The Principal has expectations and standards which are passed on and these things happen [expectations are met]'. The Principal himself stated: 'If you don't have someone 'shaking the tree', you can get the same lessons for the twentieth time'.

Another principal commented:

> I talk about performance all the time, give credit to teachers, ensure they know I am pleased.

This was confirmed by the site report for the school, which noted:

> [The Principal] is up-front and clear on expectations.

The report also noted:

> Strong and clear leadership was evident across the school. The Principal articulates the school's vision and models the characteristics of community which are ascribed to by all stakeholders.

A Deputy Principal from another school reported:

> We are here to develop clear policies and a safe and secure environment. We want to remove inconsistency faster so that everything runs smoothly. We need ways of doing things that are agreed on. There is a clear expectation that you do your job the best you can – a structure is in place and an agreed upon way of doing things ... Part of it is to supervise and help teachers set priorities so we all actively engage in a cycle of improvement and development ... What is most important is dogged persistence. Following the same procedures is important. Having documents and policies is common sense but many schools don't do it.

The Principal from the above school concurred, the research team noting:

> To [the Principal], the key to running a successful school is commitment and high expectations, particularly of the head teachers. Kids don't want to be

patronised. They want a disciplined place with rules and consequences. Over the years a school loses energy ... All schools need good structures and systems in place. Teachers should have the belief that kids can learn.

These leaders are aware of the importance and value of providing professional, pleasant facilities and of treating staff professionally, expecting a high standard of professionalism in return. Principals placed a high priority on school cleanliness and a pleasant environment. It was considered important that graffiti and mess were dealt with promptly, with gardens, seating and shade areas improved and maintained. Staff rooms, classrooms and other spaces were clean and pleasant, with resources diverted for improved furniture and fittings. These principals realised the importance of school pride, identification with the school and its reputation in the community. Students and staff responded to this and spoke in positive terms of the school. Even in the large urban schools visited by the research team, it was rare to see rubbish or evidence of vandalism.

One school encapsulated much of the above. The school was well over a century old and had a mixture of buildings from different eras. The site was a cramped one in a highly urbanised area. Prior to the appointment of the Principal, the school had been feeling the effects of competition from other schools and systems and had been in decline. However, this has been turned around and there was now pressure on facilities. The Principal (and the previous principal) had instigated refurbishment of the staff common room. The staff now referred to this as the 'Qantas Club' and they could be seen meeting and working with other staff and students in the pleasant surroundings. A cappuccino machine was installed. The old, dusty, open canteen had been walled in, rubber industrial floor covering placed over the bare concrete, and aluminium café tables and chairs installed. Pot plants had been provided and older Internet-linked computers arranged along one wall. The canteen was now in effect an Internet café and senior common room. A roster system ensured that students without home Internet access had priority use of computers. Students responded positively to this situation and graffiti and damage were minimal. Despite its large student population, the site visit team was impressed with the cleanliness of the school. The effect of all of this had been to lift both pride and expectations for behaviour in the school.

A further way vision and expectations for the school were communicated was through recognition of staff and student achievement. Principals saw and maintained teaching and learning as the central purpose of the school (see 'Focus on students, learning and teaching') and were observed to take every opportunity to recognise student and staff achievement and to 'talk up the school'. They utilised a variety of media including assemblies, newsletters, announcements, awards, letters, personal approaches, visits to classrooms and the local press. They had helped to create a positive school climate of high expectations and striving for success. They sought ways for every student to feel and be successful and for every teacher to receive appropriate recognition. Such recognition was perceived by students and staff as authentic and received in good humour. It eventually makes an impact and an upward cycle is set in motion. One site report for a central school (K–Year 10) noted:

> *When he arrived in 2000, the Principal was struck by the extent to which [School] assemblies were occasions for berating students rather than celebrating meritorious achievements. He set about reviewing the [student] welfare policy K–10 (it has been reviewed three times in the last ten years) to emphasise more of the positive aspects of the school and its students' achievements.*

The Principal of the above school commented:

> *What we've now got in place is a welfare policy that addresses the whole school needs that the community has had input to, and when you read the document, it is overwhelmingly positive. I think that has been a major change in getting people back on task. The 'woe is me' side of things is starting to change ... I noticed in my first year that the main focus of the [full school] assembly ... was to berate ... Even at the end of the year, we only had about five to nine kids achieving gold levels [for good behaviour] ... even the [School] Captains didn't achieve it, so I set about turning that around and last year we had 120 on gold and we had a big celebration.*

Another site team reported:

> *The school holds timetabled assemblies of recognition for rewarding behaviour and achievement, while the Principal holds presentation BBQs at which every student who has not been referred under the discipline system is presented with a Certificate of Appreciation. This is an innovation of the current Principal.*

'Talking up' takes place beyond the school. One site report for a school identified for exceptional outcomes in English noted:

> *The Principal ... takes every opportunity to promote the work of the teachers, citing occasions where she has shown English units [of work] at meetings of teachers held at country centres.*

It was striking how frequently principals were given credit for school improvement by staff, students and community members, yet how these principals usually attempted to deflect such praise to others. The site report for another school commented:

> *The Principal was full of praise for her 'impressive Executive' and the head teachers with whom she works. She said, 'I dread them going'. In fact, they said the same about her.*

Such generosity of spirit and lack of professional jealousy is another aspect of moral or authentic leadership, and was seen to positively influence the climate and culture of the schools concerned.

5   Teacher learning, responsibility and trust

Principals (and other leaders) were found to place a high value on teacher learning and funded staff development inside and outside the school. They modelled professional learning, being prepared to learn from teachers, students and others. They released staff to engage in professional development activities and brought others into the school to provide assistance. Principals said they 'never' turned down a legitimate and reasonable request for teacher development assistance. These principals were prepared to invest school funds to promote teachers' professional learning. This connects with a whole-school focus on students and their learning mentioned later. A site report team noted:

> *Professional development is considered to be an important component in improving the skills and knowledge of all school staff. The Principal has increased the budget for training and development across the school by more than $13,000 to $16,000 to ensure that many more teachers can be offered a chance to improve their teaching.*

The research team at another site reported:

> *The Principal gives considerable encouragement to staff to participate in professional development and several people commented on how adept she was at identifying and utilising sources of funding to enable staff to participate in professional development activity.*

While these principals rarely said no to any reasonable request for professional development, there was an expectation that those taking up these opportunities would in-service staff so that the benefits were maximised. Staff development days and meetings were often given over to providing teachers with new skills and knowledge and the confidence to try different teaching approaches. Through empowering, encouraging and supporting teachers to become learners, these leaders acknowledged and fostered the leadership of others. They respected and recognised others' capacities and achievements. They identified talent and potential and encouraged, 'coached' and supported these people, sometimes at the risk of being accused of favouritism.

They recognised that if change and improvement are to take root in the school culture, they needed to distribute responsibility and leadership capacity throughout the school and to trust people. Sharing of responsibility – as opposed to delegation – also assisted in successful leadership succession. A number of principals joked about making themselves redundant through the development of others.

A site report at a school identified for success with literacy across the curriculum noted:

> The Principal has created the context in which these programs operate. There is widespread agreement that the Principal 'allows' people to take the lead with ideas. [A staff member] said, 'We are given 'permission to play here' by the Principal – always encouraged to try things out'. One English teacher told us that 'the Principal does a lot of allowing' and she saw the Principal as having created the 'productive environment' for her to grow as a teacher.

The issue of trust and giving people 'space' was seen as an important factor in teacher development. A teacher in a school identified for outstanding outcomes in ESL commented:

> The Principal is very supportive in that he is a good leader ... if he knows we are doing our job, he doesn't interfere, but he's always there if need be. The last Principal was terrific too.

Another aspect of trust and shared responsibility is that of 'blame' when something goes wrong. These principals showed a propensity to give and share credit, but to also shoulder responsibility.

6 Student support, common purpose and collaboration

Whether the focus of the site visit was on a curriculum area or a program, it was found that student support in all its guises was central to the exceptional outcomes being achieved.

Student support was seen as broader than formal 'welfare' and 'discipline' policies and programs and was perceived as every teacher's responsibility. Student support was found to have a predominantly academic focus of 'getting students back into learning', rather than being about 'warm fuzzies', or 'enhancing self-concept', to use the words of a number of teachers interviewed. Thus, student support and academic achievement are seen not as mutually exclusive, but mutually reinforcing.[12]

Principals and other leaders facilitated the centrality of student welfare through supporting welfare teams and ensuring a common approach and commitment. Students understood and supported student welfare policies and procedures and perceived student welfare as something done *for* them, rather than *to* them. Clear communication, understanding, and consistent and 'fair' application lie at the heart of successful school welfare programs and procedures. One site team noted:

> In terms of the alignment between the Adelaide Goals, welfare is seen as the basis of everything in the school. 'Welfare allows learning to happen. There is a lot of PD on welfare, behaviour management/welfare systems. For many of the kids, we are the family and we talk about that considerably'. [Principal] ... 70 per cent of [the Principal's] time is welfare, though much is picked up by the two DPs. The background of the kids is often horrific, e.g. teachers have recently supplied heaters and mattresses for a family whose income and savings were gambled away. 'Every kid is valued', [the Principal] emphasises, and THAT drives the emphasis on literacy, welfare, numeracy, ICT. Her 'core philosophy' is that 'the needs of the kids drive the curriculum', and not the other way around.

While these schools were not Utopian, nor free of discipline and behaviour problems, a common view expressed by staff, students and community members was that student behaviour had improved over time, with commensurate positive effects on school success and reputation. The clear consensus was that 'students cannot learn until their welfare needs have been met'. Improved student behaviour creates an environment where learning can occur.[13]

In a high percentage of schools – both faculty and program sites – it was observed that principals had identified and utilised a central focus, for example ICT, assessment, literacy, pedagogy or student welfare. Programs to support and develop such areas bring members and parts of the school together, leading to better understanding and commitment and improved efficiencies and outcomes.

However, these leaders are pragmatic. They know it is impossible to gain unanimous support, approval and commitment from staff. Rather than attempting to move all staff simultaneously, they concentrate on those who are talented and committed and provide them with support (encouragement, time, resources and professional development). These pockets of staff may be within faculties or across the school. They are empowered and encouraged by the principal, who may facilitate bringing like-minded staff together. There is a danger in this, in that some staff may be left behind or be resentful and obstructive. However, it is equally true that 'if you wait for everyone to get on the bus, it will never leave'.

As part of their risk-taking approach, principals gambled that the 'contagion effects' of committed staff and demonstrated success will bring some – but probably not all – negative or reluctant people 'on-side'. One site report where English had been the focus noted:

> The Principal had offered support to all faculties for HSC planning, but English was the first to take it up and made most use of it. As a result, the Principal openly supported this Faculty in its efforts to meet the demands of the 'new' HSC.

In another school, the central focus identified to move the school forward was ESL. The report noted:

> The Principal prepared the potential for growth [in ESL] by strategic recruitment and by holding strong expectations of existing staff. If the members of staff didn't develop/grow, they were literally by-passed.

7 Focus on students, learning and teaching – the core category

The overarching theme or finding emerging from analysis of data pertaining to leadership in the schools where exceptional outcomes were found to be occurring in Years 7 to 10, was the belief that the central purpose and focus of the school is teaching and learning. These principals and their staff recognised that every effort must be made to provide an environment in which each student can experience success and academic, personal and social growth. Even in schools that had been identified for success in cross-school programs, it was apparent that there was a central focus on assisting and equipping the individual student so that he or she could succeed academically. A site team noted:

> The Head Teacher of English mentioned the support for teaching and learning provided by the Executive when she was asked why she thought [School] was selected for the AESOP project. She considered that an important factor was having a 'Principal who values core business and is enthusiastic about it'.

This view held by the Head Teacher was confirmed by the site visit team:

> The current Principal has headed [the school] for two-and-a-half years ... As Principal she has been concerned with putting 'good structures and systems' in place to support the 'core business of learning and teaching' in the classroom. The Principal reflected that she has been able to take her 'eye off the curriculum' and put in place 'frameworks for systems, so teachers are able to meet the demands of learning and teaching'.

A site report from another school noted:

> *The arrival of the current Principal in 1998 resulted in improvements in the school's success. Since 1998 there has been a schoolwide focus on teaching and learning. The Principal has undoubtedly contributed to a revival of the school's reputation and an increased focus on academic achievement.*

Principals of the schools where exceptional outcomes were being achieved were found to be relentless in their quest for enhanced student achievement. They did not become distracted and 'bogged down' by the administrative demands of the principalship, finding ways to concentrate their energies on educational leadership.

They constantly reminded students, staff and the community that the core purpose of the school was teaching and learning. Their external awareness and engagement, their bias towards innovation, their personal qualities, their vision and expectations and the climate of success that results from this, their emphasis on teacher learning, their trust of staff, and their focus on student support, common purpose and collaboration, are all geared to the facilitation of student achievement. Their focus on students, their welfare and learning, acts as a touchstone for all that happens in the school.

In schools of students from lower socio-economic backgrounds it was observed that principals and other leaders placed a high priority on the 'personal' and 'social' aspects of education with a view to creating an environment in which students could experience academic success to improve their life chances. This was consistent with their social justice agenda mentioned previously.

Principals were not mainly responsible for the exceptional educational outcomes observed, but their leadership was found to be a crucial factor in creating and sustaining an environment in which teachers can teach, students can learn, and exceptional outcomes can occur. Their influence on school climate and culture, teachers' professional learning and successful teaching was significant.

Conclusion to how school leaders promote teaching and learning

The above series of personal qualities, professional attributes, values, philosophies, approaches and actions might appear idealistic or prescriptive. I realise that this sounds like the job description and person specifications for a 'super principal', but this is what we found.

There is a danger when attributes or factors such as those outlined above are regarded as 'quick fixes' or recipes for success and the importance of school history and context are not recognised.

The fact that some of the principals and their staff had spent years reaching present levels of performance and achievement refutes the notion of easy solutions or quick responses to big challenges and problems. It was apparent, however, that it is possible to set up an upward cycle of improvement. The worrying point is that without adequate leadership succession, these hard-fought gains can quickly be dissipated. Going up is harder than going down.

Further, the attributes, actions or qualities of principals outlined in this chapter need to be considered as both product (output) and process (input) variables, in that they contribute to future change and improvement. For example, it takes time and effort to develop effective communication in a school but once this occurs, effective communication becomes an asset or resource for further improvement. In the majority, if not all of the outstanding sites, it was clear that further improvement was taking place in the context of an 'upward cycle' of success mentioned previously.

Finally, as noted in the introductory section of this chapter, the degree of influence of principals was somewhat surprising, given that the project aim was to identify and investigate faculties and teams producing outstanding educational outcomes in Years 7 to 10, rather than effective schools as a whole, or effective principals. This finding could *partly* call into question the current concentration on the individual teacher as the major within-school factor in student accomplishment. While there is little doubt about the importance of the individual teacher, based on these findings and the literature in general, principals can play key roles in creating and maintaining the conditions and environment where teachers can teach effectively and students can learn.

Chapter 4 will introduce a typology to help us understand why and how the principals and other leaders in the AESOP study were so successful in driving improvement in teaching and learning in their schools.

Acknowledgements

The ideas on leadership expressed in this chapter are mine but have been influenced by the writings and ideas of the other investigators of the AESOP study: Geoff Barnes, Paul Brock, Bill Green, David Laird, John Pegg, Wayne Sawyer and Robert Stevens. The contribution of the AESOP series editor A. Ross Thomas and others involved with site visits and reports is also acknowledged.

Notes
1 Dinham, S., & Rowe, K. (2007). *Teaching and learning in middle schooling: A review of the literature. Report to the New Zealand Ministry of Education.* Camberwell: ACER.

2. MCEETYA. (1999). *The Adelaide Declaration on National Goals for Schooling in the Twenty-first Century*. Canberra: Ministerial Council on Education, Employment, Training and Youth Affairs.
3. Dinham, S. (2007). The secondary head of department and the achievement of exceptional student outcomes. *Journal of Educational Administration*, 45(1), 62–79; Dinham, S. (2005). Principal leadership for outstanding educational outcomes. *Journal of Educational Administration*, 43(4), 338–356.
4. All published (2007). Teneriffe, Qld: Post Pressed.
5. Dinham, S. (2007). The secondary head of department and the achievement of exceptional student outcomes. *Journal of Educational Administration*, 45(1), 62–79.
6. Dinham, S. (2007). *Leadership for exceptional educational outcomes*. Teneriffe, Qld: Post Pressed.
7. QSR. (2002). *NUD*IST 6*. Melbourne: QSR International.
8. Strauss, A., & Corbin, J. (1990). *Basics of qualitative research – Grounded theory procedures and techniques*. Newbury Park, CA: Sage.
9. Dinham, S., & Scott, C. (2000). Moving into the third, outer domain of teacher satisfaction. *Journal of Educational Administration*, 38(4), 379–396.
10. Duignan, P., & Bhindi, N. (1997). Leadership for a new century: Authenticity, intentionality, spirituality, and sensibility. *Educational Management and Administration*, 25(2), 117–132.
11. Hargreaves, A., & Fink, D. (2004). The seven principles of sustainable leadership. *Educational Leadership*, 61(7), 8–13.
12. Scott, C., & Dinham, S. (2005). Parenting, teaching and self-esteem. *The Australian Educational Leader*, 27(1), 28–30; Dinham, S., & Scott, C. (2007). Parenting, teaching and leadership styles. *The Australian Educational Leader*, 29(1), 30–32; 45.
13. Hattie, J. (2007). Developing potentials for learning: Evidence, assessment, and progress, EARLI Biennial Conference, Budapest, Hungary. Available at: http://www.education.auckland.ac.nz/uoa/education/staff/j.hattie/presentations.cfm

4 | Responsive and demanding teaching and leadership

If you are on the wrong road, progress means doing an about-turn and walking back to the right road; and in that case, the man [sic] who turns back soonest is the most progressive man. Going back is the quickest way on.
(C.S. Lewis)

Introduction

The successful teachers described in Chapter 2 and the leaders of schools achieving exceptional student outcomes in Chapter 3 shared a number of attributes. Members of each study had high-level interpersonal skills and personal qualities that were admired. They had earned a high degree of credibility and their relations with others were characterised by mutual respect and trust. Their expectations for staff and students were high, but so too were their expectations for themselves. They set a good example through moral authority and strongly believed in what they were doing. Each made teaching and learning their main priority, with students the central focus.

The above philosophy of 'give a lot, expect a lot' was particularly marked in schools from areas of lower socio-economic status. There is a tendency to dichotomise schools as being either of 'welfare' or 'academic' types. In welfare schools, there are frequently lower expectations, with an emphasis on inculcating 'social' and 'living' skills and boosting student self-esteem at the expense of academic achievement, yet in the two projects it was evident that the function of student welfare in the disadvantaged or lower socio-economic status schools was more about 'getting students back into learning' for their future benefit than making students feel good about themselves.

In helping to understand this situation, Catherine Scott and I have used the work of Diana Baumrind to provide a conceptual framework for analysis. We believe that Baumrind's work on parenting styles has strong resonance and utility for understanding both quality teaching and effective leadership.

As a postscript, I also apply Baumrind's typology more broadly to educational change since the 1960s, before finishing this chapter with a case study from a popular Australian television series, *Summer Heights High*.

Parenting styles

Intuitively, parenting and teaching appear to have a lot in common. Each involves attempting to meet children's needs and providing guidance for their development. Both parents and teachers have a high level of duty of care as older, wiser adults placed in a position of responsibility and authority. Each has a nurturing aspect, coupled with control and guidance, hopefully leading to maturity of thought and action, self-confidence and autonomy for the young people concerned, so that they can make a place for themselves in society and lead fulfilling lives.

Equally apparent is the fact that there are different styles of parenting and teaching. A key question then, is that of whether some styles of parenting and teaching are more effective than others in meeting the needs and expectations of children and society. A related issue is that of the degree to which parents and teachers should be authority figures, and the degree to which they should attempt to meet children's needs.

The consequences for children of what have been called different styles of parenting have been the subject of considerable research since the late 1960s, beginning with the work of Diana Baumrind.[1]

According to Baumrind, two dimensions underlie parenting style: *responsiveness* and *demandingness*. Each considers the nature of the parent–child relationship.

- *Responsiveness*, also described as warmth or supportiveness, is defined as 'the extent to which parents intentionally foster individuality, self-regulation and assertion by being attuned, supportive, and acquiescent to children's special needs and demands'.
- *Demandingness* (or behavioural control) refers to 'the claims parents make on children to become integrated into the family whole, by their maturity demands, supervision, disciplinary efforts and willingness to confront the child who disobeys'.[2]

By considering the two dimensions of responsiveness and demandingness and whether each is low or high, four parenting styles have been proposed:

1. *Uninvolved:* low responsiveness, low demandingness
2. *Authoritarian:* low responsiveness, high demandingness
3. *Permissive:* high responsiveness, low demandingness
4. *Authoritative:* high responsiveness, high demandingness

Based upon the research of Baumrind and later work by others, the following profiles for each of the four types are provided.

1 Uninvolved parenting

Uninvolved parents are low on both demandingness and responsiveness. They may feed and clothe their children but show little interest in them, either to display warmth and affection or to discipline them and provide structure and consistent expectations. Uninvolved parents are frequently living in difficult circumstances that overwhelm their capacity to be sensitive and supportive towards their children. Children from uninvolved parents and homes tend to fare poorly in all domains of development. Extreme forms of uninvolved parenting are neglect and abandonment or 'failing to provide the necessities of life', as it is termed in some jurisdictions.

2 Authoritarian parenting

Authoritarian parents are high on demandingness and expect obedience from children 'because I say so'. They may inflict punishment when compliance is not forthcoming. They attempt to instil traditional values, such as obedience and respect for authority. They are also low on responsiveness and do not consult or negotiate with children about expectations, nor display much warmth towards them.

This style of parenting is regarded these days as 'old-fashioned' and when people wish to make unflattering comparisons between old and new style teaching it is an authoritarian style that is generally claimed to characterise teachers from the 'bad old days' of 'chalk and talk'.

Children from authoritarian homes tend to perform well at school and tend not to become involved in problem behaviour. However, they also tend to have poorer social skills, lower self-esteem, and to be more prone to emotional problems, including depression. Not surprisingly, some children of authoritarian parenting will later rebel or 'break free'.

3 Permissive parenting

In direct contrast to authoritarian parents are permissive parents, who are low on demandingness and high on responsiveness. Permissive parents are accepting and affirming of the child's impulses, desires and actions. They consult with the child about family decisions and give explanations for rules while making few demands for household responsibility and orderly behaviour. The permissive parent is a resource for the child but not an active agent responsible for shaping or altering ongoing or future behaviour. The permissive parent allows the child to regulate his or her own activities as much as possible, avoids the exercise of control, and does not encourage him or her to obey externally defined standards. Permissive parents attempt to use reason but not overt power to accomplish parental ends.

Children reared permissively tend to have high self-esteem, are generally cheerful and positive in outlook, and are more creative than their peers. So far, so good. However, they also tend to do poorly at school, to lack persistence at challenging tasks, to be unpopular with their peers because of poor social skills and to be spontaneously rebellious and dependent in their relations with parents and other adults. They are also much more likely than their peers, raised by authoritarian parents, to be involved in antisocial and/or illegal acts.

4 Authoritative parenting

In contrast to both the permissive and the authoritarian styles, authoritative parents are high on both responsiveness and demandingness. They are warm and supportive of their children, aware of their current developmental needs and sensitive to meeting these needs. They also, however, have high expectations and set appropriate limits while providing structure and consistent rules, the reasons for which they explain to their child, rather than simply expecting unthinking obedience. While they maintain adult authority, they are also willing to listen to their child and to negotiate rules and situations.

This combination of sensitivity, caring, high expectations and structure has been shown to have the best consequence for children, who commonly display high academic achievement, good social skills, moral maturity, autonomy and high self-esteem.

Teaching and parenting styles

In our original paper on parenting and teaching styles we stated how we believed this typology had relevance to understanding teaching today.[3]

Not surprisingly, because of the numerous parallels evident between parenting and teaching, we were advocating for an authoritative teaching style. This was based upon findings from various research projects with which we had been involved, including those cited previously, and our experience with beginning teachers, many of whom appeared to subscribe to a permissive model of teaching (see below).

Among other lessons from application of Baumrind's typology to teaching, we were very interested with the notion of building student self-esteem. There is a popular view that boosting student self-esteem can lead to a range of desirable outcomes. Conversely, too low self-esteem is believed to lead to problematic outcomes for the individual concerned. The argument also goes that students from minority and lower socio-economic backgrounds will tend to have lower self-esteem and need to feel better about themselves if they are to be successful. Boosting or increasing their self-esteem is thus desirable.

Previously Catherine Scott and I were each involved with teacher pre-service education at several universities. The bulk of our pre-service teachers came to us with a strong interest in children and a desire to help them grow and thrive. Along with this 'caring for kids' ethos, they frequently expressed a strong aversion to being in a relationship of authority over children.

The general social distrust of anyone in a position of authority has made its way into students' value systems, as has the idea of the teacher as the 'guide by the side' who facilitates children's learning and their self-actualisation. Our student teachers also articulated the view that the supreme duty of the teacher is to foster self-esteem, which they believe will inevitably lead to other desirable outcomes such as academic achievement and kind and considerate behaviour. This desire is accompanied by fear that higher demands, competition, 'failure', criticism and expectations that challenge children may damage their self-esteem, because not all will be able to meet these expectations. Instead, learning must be 'fun' and relevant, and so effortless that children 'hardly feel it happening', to quote one of our pre-service students.

Our teacher pre-service students then would like their future pupils to be confident and independent learners ('lifelong learners', to use the popular term), with high self-esteem, but also to work cooperatively with others. Can what we know about parenting help to decide the best way to aid pupils to become the best people that they can? Is a teaching style that aims to facilitate learning and development while avoiding asserting authority over children, likely to result in future citizens who display all the virtues listed above?

To respond to these questions, the comparison between permissive and authoritative parenting suggests that self-esteem is not the cause of anything; rather it is the consequence of having warm and responsive parents and presumably teachers. It can co-occur with either the desirable traits of the authoritatively reared child or with the less desirable attributes of the permissively parented young person.

What makes the difference for good and not so good outcomes is the level of demandingness that the child has also experienced. High expectations, clear rules, appropriately enforced adult authority and consistent structure make the difference between the autonomous, mature, responsible young person and the rebellious, whining, socially inept – to use your grandmother's term – 'spoilt' child.

Those who have seen the television series *Brat Camp* will recognise the problems associated with a permissive style of parenting. In the series, rebellious, 'spoilt' adolescents from the United Kingdom are sent to a desert in the United States for a period of months where the aim is to provide the demandingness which has been lacking in their upbringing to this point.

Totally unused to compliance with authority, structure and direction, these young people find it hard-going, coming up against staff who are well-trained and unbending in their demands for discipline and acceptable, responsible behaviour.

In their home situations, the parents of these children had been unable or unwilling to institute any form of guidance or control and had resorted in many cases to buying their son's or daughter's compliance. These young people responded to this permissive, indulgent parenting style by being verbally and in some cases physically abusive to their parents and engaging in various forms of anti-social, self-destructive and illegal behaviour.

Not surprisingly, many had experienced problems at school and were basically dysfunctional young people. The 'tough love' approach demonstrated in *Brat Camp* is shown to be successful with the majority of these young people, with the transformation in their relationship with others, and their feelings about themselves, quite pronounced. For some, however, the process fails and they revert to their previous patterns of behaviour. Obviously, such remedies are expensive, time-consuming and beyond the means of most families.

Sometimes there is a feeling in schools that a choice has to be made between concentrating on students' welfare – responsiveness – and a focus on learning achievement – demandingness. Lessons drawn from research literature on school and teacher effectiveness and parenting styles suggest that the best outcomes are achieved where both responsiveness and demandingness are the focus of school policies and procedures.

Research from the AESOP study detailed in the previous chapter confirmed the existence of a belief in the welfare and academic dichotomy amongst some teachers and schools, yet the study findings refuted the truth of this. Schools where exceptional academic or subject outcomes were being achieved were found to have highly effective student welfare practices and programs underpinning this academic success. On the other hand, at schools where the existence of exceptional outcomes in cross-school programs were identified, the main function of these programs was to 'get students back into learning' – 'we are not interested in "warm fuzzies" or self-concept', as a number of teachers involved with welfare programs noted.

The AESOP study confirmed that it is not a matter of circumstances or choice whether a school is a 'welfare' school, or one where academic achievement is prized. Both aspects are vital to student success. What tends to happen in practice, however, is that certain students (Indigenous, low socio-economic status, non-English-speaking background) are categorised and stigmatised. Teachers have low expectations for these students, and in some cases for their whole school. It is thought that the best thing for these students is to keep them off the streets, teach them the basics and boost their self-esteem through special treatment.

In the best schools, however, there is a focus on students *and* their learning, and all students can experience success; self-efficacy and achievement being the best builders of self-esteem and confidence.

Applying the typology to educational leadership

After applying Baumrind's typology of parenting styles to what we know about teaching, we then turned our attention to educational leadership.[4] In considering the findings of a range of research projects focusing to various degrees on quality teaching, educational leadership (including distributive leadership) and teachers' professional learning,[5] we found that the four types of parenting and teaching can be productively applied to educational leadership, given the central role relationships play in the practice of leadership. As with any typology, the four prototypes are 'extremes' unlikely to be found in the ideal form, but assist in our understanding of reality. No one is totally demanding or totally responsive, and not even a single-celled organism is totally lacking in either responsiveness or demandingness towards its environment.

What then might each broad type of leadership look like, based upon the findings of the above research projects? It should be noted that these types of leadership have been observed at all levels within schools and in educational hierarchies. My guess is that as you read the profile of each, you will be mentally allocating people of your acquaintance to each type.

Note: The term 'organisation' is sometimes used in the following discussion to cover the various domains of the leader (faculty, department or team, school, etc.)

RESPONSIVENESS

```
                    Low              →              High
          High ┌─────────────────┬─────────────────┐
   D          │                 │                 │
   E          │  Authoritarian  │  Authoritative  │
   M          │   leadership    │   leadership    │
   A          │                 │                 │
   N          │                 │                 │
   D          │                 │                 │
   I       ↑  ├─────────────────┼─────────────────┤
   N          │                 │                 │
   G          │                 │                 │
   N          │   Uninvolved    │   Permissive    │
   E          │   leadership    │   leadership    │
   S          │                 │                 │
   S          │                 │                 │
          Low └─────────────────┴─────────────────┘
```

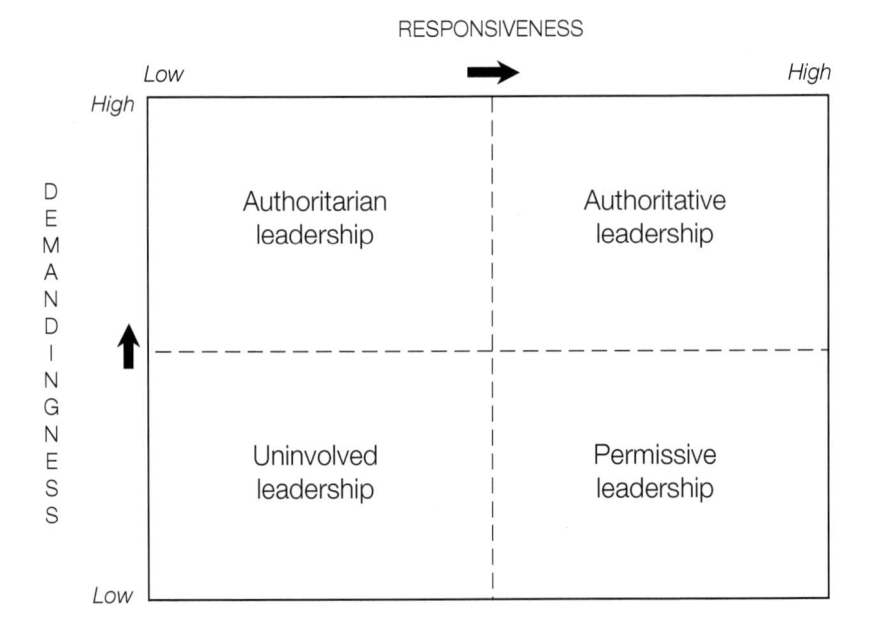

Figure 4.1 Four prototypes of leadership (Dinham & Scott, after Baumrind)

1 Uninvolved leadership

The uninvolved leader is low in both responsiveness and demandingness towards others and practises leadership by abrogation or neglect. He or she makes little impact of a positive nature on the school, its performance or its culture. The uninvolved leader can be an effective administrator and may rationalise his or her lack of educational leadership through the piles of papers with which he or she deals. Alternatively, the uninvolved leader may be overwhelmed by his or her situation.

Under uninvolved leadership staff are left to their own devices with few demands made upon them, and they receive little direction or support. Positive and negative feedback and recognition tend to be lacking. Students and staff perceive such leaders as remote, and uninvolved leaders tend to have a low profile in the community and wider profession. Few know them well.

Standards and expectations from the uninvolved leader are not clearly articulated and are possibly too low. The resultant inconsistency and uncertainty can lead to confusion, conflict and poor organisational performance.

Insufficient attention and direction may be given to key organisational functions such as planning, policies, recruitment and induction, systems, communication and evaluation. The values and norms of the organisation may be unclear.[6]

Under uninvolved leadership, the school or department is reactive, drifting and possibly sinking. 'Balkanisation' and 'groupthink' (see Chapter 7) can flourish in this leadership vacuum and sub-groups can push the organisation into dangerous areas. Other leaders and groups may attempt to keep the organisation afloat and on course, but this is difficult without support from the top.

While good things can happen in individual classes and within teams of teachers, the organisation is neither a true learning community nor close to reaching its potential. Schools and departments operating under uninvolved educational leadership are thus sub-optimal in their performance.

2   Authoritarian leadership

Authoritarian leaders are high on demandingness and expect compliance from all concerned. They have a traditional conception of leadership based on obedience and respect for positional authority and status. They tend not to negotiate or consult with staff, students or the community, but expect their orders to be obeyed without question.

Reflecting their low responsiveness, authoritarian leaders focus on procedures rather than people. Because of their use of rules, punishments and sanctions, they may be feared, rather than respected or liked. Recognition and positive feedback from the authoritative leader are lacking, although people may occasionally receive a blast from the leader as he or she reinforces control and authority through pulling people back into line and reminding them who is the boss.

Standards and expectations of the authoritarian leader may be high and are reinforced by extrinsic mechanisms. Control, consistency and order are emphasised at the expense of flexibility and compassion. Rules, 'going by the book' and equal treatment for all override adaptability.

Schools and departments of authoritarian leaders may be orderly and well run with delegation, reporting and accountability systems utilised to facilitate this. There tends to be a high degree of dependency on the authoritarian leader who has the final say on everything. Organisations led by authoritarian leaders can be characterised by low risk taking and innovation.

There may be considerable untapped potential in organisations led by authoritarian leaders. Staff and students can be infantilised under the authoritarian leader.

Some will appreciate the uncompromising stance and strength of the authoritarian leader (including novice or less able teachers who need structure), while others will feel stifled and frustrated by their lack of input to the organisation and lack of opportunities to exercise leadership (including expert teachers who desire autonomy).[7]

There may be a leadership vacuum with the departure of the authoritarian leader because of staff dependency and the leader's failure to practise distributive leadership and develop staff capacity.

3 Permissive leadership

Permissive leaders are by definition the opposite of the authoritarian leader. They are more responsive than demanding. Permissive leaders may have good people skills and are open and responsive to the needs and wishes of others. Permissive leaders may spend much of their time being available.

As permissive leaders value the input of others, planning and decision making can take quite some time. Permissive leaders tend to use reason and consensus building rather than direction and authority, and the permissive leader may find it difficult to be decisive.

Permissive leaders allow staff and students a high degree of discretion and even indulgence, but a lack of direction and accountability can prove counter-productive. The trust and leeway permissive leaders extend to others can be exploited. The permissive leader may demonstrate a reluctance or incapacity to intervene or confront, leaving it to others to work out a solution. Small problems can become bigger under the permissive leader.

Standards and expectations can be unclear, contradictory and too low. The permissive leader is undemanding and may make allowances for those who transgress or fail to deliver. Again, some will exploit this.

Schools led by permissive leaders can be characterised by organisational looseness and a lack of clarity and consistency in the application of systems and procedures.

There may be a lack of individual and collective responsibility resulting in a degree of disorder and even disobedience and chaos as people 'do their own thing'. The permissive leader may frequently change his or her mind, depending upon the last person he or she has spoken with. Permissive leaders often use covert, 'special' deals to obtain or 'buy' cooperation. Lack of transparency in decision making can thus be a problem with permissive leadership.

Some self-directed teachers and groups of teachers will flourish under a permissive leadership regime, while others will drift through lack of direction or worse, avoid responsibility. Others will take the opportunity to build a power base.

While schools led by permissive leaders can be happy, sociable places, this may be at the expense of progress and achievement as the permissive leader attempts to keep everyone on side.

4 Authoritative leadership

Authoritative leaders share the positive attributes of permissive and authoritarian types. They are responsive, warm and supportive. They are sensitive to the diversity of individual and collective needs and are inclusive. They are good listeners and collaboratively build consensus and commitment. They tend to be good networkers with a high profile beyond the school. They are aware of and responsive to the environment within and outside the school.

Authoritative leaders are also demanding. They are clear in their expectations of themselves, staff and students. They communicate high standards and set an example that others seek to emulate. They are assertive, without overreliance on the rules and sanctions of the authoritarian leader. Authoritative leaders 'give a lot and expect a lot'. People say they don't want to let the authoritative leader down. The personal qualities of the authoritative leader are admired by most, but not always by all. They rely more on moral than positional authority.

Authoritative leaders exercise their authority appropriately and in a timely fashion. They know when to consult and when to be decisive. They have the skills to work with others and the courage to act alone.

Authoritative leaders put students and their learning at the centre of the school. They seek ways for every student to experience success and to achieve. They see student welfare as essential to academic success and oversee clear and effective welfare policies and procedures.

Authoritative leaders give timely and appropriate feedback, both positive and negative. People know where they stand with the authoritative leader.

Authoritative leaders place a strong emphasis on professional learning and are prepared to invest in this inside and outside the school. They model professional learning for others. People have the opportunity and encouragement to flourish under authoritative leadership. The authoritative leader seeks to develop competent, assertive, self-regulated staff and students.

These leaders possess a vision for the future development of the school which they communicate clearly. They tend to have a bias towards innovation and action, and practise distributive leadership rather than line management delegation. Other staff are encouraged, entrusted and supported to develop new programs, policies and practices. The professionalism and capabilities of others are recognised and the authoritative leader is able to release untapped potential in individuals and the organisation as a whole.

Authoritative leaders are strategic and realise the impossibility of moving a whole staff forward simultaneously; as noted, if one 'waits for everyone to get aboard the bus, it will never leave'. They thus empower individuals and groups, hoping for a contagion or groundswell effect. Through influence and action, the authoritative leader moves people out of their comfort zones.

Schools led by authoritative leaders tend to move and improve through an emphasis on continual evaluation, evidence, planning and action. Even when change is externally imposed, authoritative leaders find ways to use this to the school's advantage.

Overall, authoritative leaders have a positive influence on school climate and culture. Authoritative leaders build leadership capacity and provide for leadership sustainability and effective leadership succession when they depart.

An important point to note is that the authoritative leaders may well vary the 'mix' of responsiveness and demandingness depending on the situation. They may, for example, be more or less demanding or responsive with certain groups or at certain stages of the organisation's development.

The vast majority of leaders encountered in the AESOP study could be readily classified as being of the authoritative type.

Conclusion to discussion of educational leadership styles

The above analysis, arising from the findings of a range of recent research projects, is premised on the notion that educational leadership is heavily dependent upon relationships.

Michael Fullan, a prolific writer on educational change, has noted:[8]

> ... we have found that the single factor common to every successful change initiative is that relationships improve. If relationships improve, things get better. If they remain the same or get worse, ground is lost. Thus leaders must be consummate relationship builders with diverse people and groups – especially with people different than themselves.

Authoritative leaders and teachers are 'relationship' people, able to 'read' and respond to others. They understand people and they understand change, which they help others to appreciate and come to grips with. They are authentic leaders, in that they model those qualities, attributes and behaviours they expect of others.

Authoritative leaders rely more on moral than positional authority, and influence more than overt control. In their relationships with teachers and students, authoritative leaders balance a high degree of responsiveness with a high degree of demandingness.

As noted, these leaders place a high priority on professional learning, which they perceive as key to changing people, practices and performance.

In many of the schools visited as part of the research projects cited previously, the most telling indicator of the power of authoritative leadership – exhibiting both high responsiveness and high demandingness – was that departments and whole schools had been turned around with commensurate improvement in student performance indicators. Schools and faculties formerly in decline were thriving with school leaders having to cope with a new problem of excessive demand for limited student places. In other cases, new leaders took schools and faculties that had plateaued at an acceptable level of performance, to higher levels of achievement.

To offer a cautionary note, the AESOP study found that the 'turning around' and 'lifting up' processes can take around six to seven years to accomplish, although some improvements can occur almost immediately.[9]

Those looking for and advocating quick fixes for struggling schools need to consider the intense, coordinated effort and teamwork, and professional learning under authoritative forms of leadership that such improvement requires. However, the evidence is clear that it can be done. As one research participant commented in the AESOP study, 'in this school we make plans now, not excuses'.

Education from the early 1960s to today: Where we went wrong

At this point, I want to introduce an analysis and argument that some of you may find confronting or disturbing.

In the early 1960s, I think it is accurate to say that 'traditional' education in much of the 'western' world was characterised by high demandingness and low responsiveness; that is, an authoritarian relationship existed between schools and students. This was certainly the case where I went to school.

There was a major emphasis on discipline, to the extent that corporal punishment and expulsion were not uncommon. There was little attempt to differentiate curricula, which were largely fixed with little flexibility for teachers and students and accompanied by a range of public and internal examinations. Post-compulsory retention rates were lower than now and students who didn't perform or conform were 'encouraged' to leave school. Homes and the community generally were also more 'traditional' or authoritarian, and parents generally backed the school and its teachers without questioning too much how the school operated, part of a general respect for institutions and authority.

During the 1960s, however, a wave of questioning of tradition, accepted practices and authority swept the western world. This was an era of protest and far-reaching social change. This change was reflected in, and in turn influenced by, changing thinking in teacher preparation and schooling, which came more under the influence of 'progressivism'.

Quite rightly, there was a feeling at this time that schools needed to respond more to students as people and to better cater for their individual backgrounds and needs. We recognised that we increasingly lived in a multicultural, diverse and changing society.

Education academics, system officials and teachers questioned established school organisational and teaching practices and over the following decades curriculum prescription and testing gave way to school-based curriculum development. Some external and internal examinations were removed and replaced with other forms of assessment. Students, like many members of society, began to speak up and engage in various forms of questioning, protest and activism.

Social concerns such as pollution and environmental degradation, racism, sexism, drugs, sexual health and awareness, nuclear warfare, militarism and multi-nationalism found a place in school curricula. Values education became prominent.

As noted, many of these developments were desirable and even overdue and were part of schools becoming more responsive to students.

However, *a fundamental error of perception occurred at this time that has ramifications to this day.*

Using the benefit of hindsight and applying the typology developed by Baumrind retrospectively, I believe that *demandingness and responsiveness were falsely dichotomised.*

Ideologically, it was thought that any increase in responsiveness towards students should be accompanied by, and in fact required, a decrease in demandingness: to be responsive was to be progressive; to be demanding was to be traditional.

Over time, schools and schooling became more responsive to *and* less demanding of students; that is, more permissive, with commensurate effects on matters such as standards, behaviour, expectations, teaching methods and the balance of the curriculum. Other false dichotomies have also reflected the polarisation of ideologies in education over this period: knowledge versus skills; learning processes versus subject content; competition versus collaboration; progressivism versus conservatism; subjects versus thematic approaches; 'guide by the side' versus 'sage on the stage' teaching, and so forth.[10]

I believe that the false dichotomisation of demandingness with responsiveness has contributed to many of the problems we see in schools today, problems which include:

- student disengagement due to lower expectations and failure to challenge and extend students

- behavioural problems through lack of, or inconsistent, guidance, standards and discipline; general lack of self-discipline
- teacher role conflict and ambiguity – activator, facilitator?; 'guide', 'sage'?
- downgrading of teacher expertise and status and de-professionalisation of teaching
- denigration of 'teacher direction' of students and forms of more explicit teaching
- overuse of student discovery and inquiry-based learning approaches[11]
- fear of harm to students arising from 'competition' and failure; lack of honesty in assessment and feedback
- learning must be 'relevant' and 'fun'; 'dumbing-down', and grade inflation
- self-esteem boosting in isolation from achievement.

These phenomena need to be considered in the context of societal changes outlined previously, including families and society being generally less authoritarian and more permissive, and adolescence and young adulthood being spread over a longer period.

When problems such as those above occur, there is a tendency to conclude that responsiveness has not gone far enough and is still being hindered by too high demandingness. Thus, problems are further exacerbated as 'more fuel is put on the fire' in the efforts of schools to be more responsive and less demanding.

There has been something of a reaction to this situation in recent times, with recognition by some that things have gone too far, but the false dichotomising of responsiveness and demandingness remains problematic. It is difficult to re-introduce higher levels of demandingness when students and teachers have become accustomed to a different regime. (See previous references to *Brat Camp*.)

In Australia, there has been a steady drift of students to the non-government sector over recent decades. In some cases, this is because parents are looking for certain values they perceive to be lacking or insufficiently emphasised in government schools. Non-government schools are thought to provide greater discipline (demandingness), while being more attuned to students' needs (responsiveness). There are no doubt other reasons for this shift, but the crux of the matter appears to be that many in the community perceive non-government schools to be more 'authoritative' than their government school counterparts, which are seen as more 'permissive', or even verging on the 'uninvolved'.

As a result, it is apparent that many government schools in Australia are attempting to emulate what some believe they see in the private sector: greater emphasis on discipline (students can be moved on if they fail to comply), wearing of school uniform, greater respect for teachers and other adults, higher standards of self-discipline and behaviour and a better quality peer group. This argument is yet another dichotomy and is, of course, grossly unfair. It is just as dangerous and fallacious to generalise about all government schools as it is to stereotype all non-government schools. The schools in the AESOP study were all government schools and the vast majority were of the authoritative type, as we have observed.

Some who speak out about this situation of lesser demandingness and greater responsiveness in schools (and society) are painted as traditionalists who are part of a 'back to basics' movement; that is, seeking more authoritarianism as in the early 1960s.

However, the best teachers, educational leaders and schools today exhibit both high demandingness and high responsiveness; that is, the relationship between schools, teachers, leaders and students is authoritative. In fact, this has probably always been the case, as it has been with parenting.

In this respect, more authoritative approaches to teaching and leadership actually represent a move towards a more desirable status quo, authoritative schooling, rather than a step backwards to authoritarianism.

A case study: The lesson of Jonah

You may have had the opportunity to see *Summer Heights High*, Chris Lilley's wonderful and thought-provoking series on ABC television in Australia. If you haven't seen the series, it is worth seeking out.

One of the central characters, Jonah, struck a particular chord with me. Here is a piece I wrote which touches on the issues I have raised above, as well as the fundamental importance of literacy. It represents my interpretation of issues raised in the series. The paper has been reprinted many times and must have struck its own chord.

The lesson of Jonah[12]

In the final episode of Chris Lilley's *Summer Heights High* we saw Jonah, the smart-arse Tongan break-dancer, dragged from the school. School was the source of much of Jonah's identity and his problems.

Like many, Jonah was always up against it. His family background was literacy poor. Reading material was lacking in the home and Jonah wasn't read to as a young child. Jonah didn't attend pre-school and by the time he entered primary he was already two to three years behind some of his peers in literacy development. This gap widened. Jonah moved from school to school and each transition had a negative effect on his learning. Jonah was one of many and his teachers, well meaning and under pressure, didn't diagnose or deal with his literacy problems.

Jonah didn't receive the individual attention, explicit teaching and feedback he needed. Jonah's lack of progress was attributed to his poor behaviour and attitude but his behaviour and attitude were largely a product of his lack of academic achievement.

Jonah couldn't master literacy and because so much of schooling is literacy based, he struggled in all curriculum areas. He knew he was falling behind and covered his inadequacy with bravado and over-confidence. Jonah avoided engaging with schoolwork as much as possible. He discovered he could make people laugh.

By the time he entered high school, Jonah was five years behind some of his peers. By year 8, he was seven years behind many in his year and found basic school work beyond him. His reading and writing skills were at year 3 level, lower than they had been in year 6. Jonah was going backwards.

Fortunately, Jonah was good at break-dancing, something which became central in his life. Unfortunately, break-dancing also got him into trouble at school and was used as a means to punish Jonah when his behaviour got out of hand.

Jonah was placed in a special reading program where he received attention and encouragement but not the tools to master literacy. It was thought that recognising and valuing his cultural background through programs such as 'Polynesian Pathways' would motivate Jonah and his friends and develop feelings of self-worth, but the program itself had no depth, consisting of grass skirts and dancing, rather than knowledge and appreciation of Polynesia's rich cultures. Jonah's real issue wasn't with his cultural background – he was distinctive for other reasons. Jonah lacked the basics, but he wasn't challenged either.

When Jonah was cooperative and well-behaved, his teachers told themselves their strategies were working but a lack of academic progress made conflict inevitable. The brighter year 7 boys discovered they could wind up Jonah and get him into trouble. In all of this, Jonah's home background was a hindrance. An absent mother and an authoritarian, unresponsive father who couldn't help him with his work didn't support Jonah's development and learning. Threats to send Jonah back to Tonga failed to improve his literacy and schoolwork.

Jonah had a growing, 'bad' reputation and was backed deeper into a corner. The frustrations and incidents became more frequent. He was suspended, which was meant to teach him a lesson. Jonah came back to school even further behind. The cut and paste work he had done while on suspension was ridiculed. After more incidents, he was expelled, physically. Jonah had failed school, and school had failed Jonah, but he didn't want to leave. It was all he had. His final act was to deface the school and the teachers' cars.

Jonah would soon come to the attention of another set of authority figures and his education would continue on the streets and in other institutions. He would be backed into other corners.

If he was lucky, however, his father or others might take an interest in him and give Jonah the guidance and warmth he needed. He might obtain an unskilled job and experience a sense of achievement and independence. Self-realisation might dawn. One day, he might even learn to read and write. At last resort, there are some good literacy programs in prison.

One day, Jonah might even be able to break the illiteracy cycle with his own children, although going 'up' to the school on their behalf would always be difficult.

Acknowledgements

Catherine Scott provided the insight to apply Baumrind's typology of parenting styles to teaching. We then developed this thinking to apply the typology to educational leadership and leadership generally.[13] This chapter is based mainly on two of our papers, along with findings from the various studies cited.[14] The final section came from my further thinking using the typology and the piece on Jonah from thinking about these matters at the time the series was aired.

Notes

1. See, for example, Baumrind, D. (1989). Rearing competent children. In Damon, W. (Ed.), *Child development today and tomorrow* (pp. 349–378). San Francisco: Jossey-Bass.
2. Baumrind, D. (1991). The influence of parenting style on adolescent competence and substance abuse. *Journal of Early Adolescence*, 11(1), 62.
3. Scott, C., & Dinham, S. (2005). Parenting, teaching and self esteem. *The Australian Educational Leader*, 27(1), 28–30.
4. Dinham, S., & Scott, C. (2007). Parenting, teaching and leadership styles, *The Australian Educational Leader*, 29(1), 30–32; 45.
5. Aubusson, P., Brady, L., & Dinham, S. (2005). *Action learning: What works? A research report prepared for the New South Wales Department of Education and Training.* Sydney: University of Technology Sydney; Ayres, P., Dinham, S., & Sawyer, W. (1999). *Successful teaching in the NSW Higher School Certificate.* Sydney: NSW Department of Education and Training; Dinham, S. (2002). NSW

quality teaching awards – Research, rigour and transparency. *Unicorn, 28*(1), 5–9; Dinham, S. (2007). The dynamics of creating and sustaining learning communities. *Unicorn Online Refereed Article No. 43*, Australian College of Educators; Dinham, S. (2007). *Leadership for exceptional educational outcomes.* Teneriffe, Qld: Post Pressed; Dinham, S., Buckland, C., Callingham, R., & Mays, H. (2005). Investigation of the factors responsible for the superior performance of male students in standardised testing at one primary school. Paper presented to the Australian Association for Research in Education, Annual Conference, Sydney, 27 November–1 December; Dinham, S., Aubusson, P., & Brady, L. (2008). Distributed leadership as a factor in and outcome of teacher action learning. *International Electronic Journal for Leadership in Learning, 12*(4). Available at: http://www.ucalgary.ca/~iejll/volume12/dinham.htm
6 Schlechty, P. (2005). *Creating great schools: Six critical systems at the heart of educational innovation.* San Francisco: Jossey-Bass.
7 Dreyfus, S., & Dreyfus, H. (1980). *A five-stage model of the mental activities involved in directed skills acquisition* (pp. 1–18). Operations Research Center, University of California, Berkeley.
8 Fullan, M. (2001). *Leading in a culture of change* (p. 5). San Francisco: Jossey-Bass.
9 Dinham, S. (2007d). How schools get moving and keep improving: Leadership for teacher learning, student success and school renewal. *Australian Journal of Education, 51*(3), 263–275.
10 Dinham, S. (2006). Teaching and teacher education: Some observations, reflections and possible solutions. *ED Ventures, 2*, 3–20.
11 Mayer, R. (2004). Should there be a three-strikes rule against pure Discovery Learning? *American Psychologist, 59*(1), 14–19.
12 See for example: Dinham, S. (2007). The lesson of Jonah. *Education Review, 17*(8), 5; Dinham, S. (2007). The (literacy) lessons of Jonah. *Australian Education Digest, 1(35)*. Available at: http://www.acsso.org.au/AED071128.pdf
13 Dinham, S. (2007). Authoritative leadership, Action learning and student accomplishment. *Conference Proceedings*, Australian Council for Educational Research, 2007 Research Conference, 33–39; Dinham, S., & Scott, C. (2008). Responsive, demanding leadership. *Management Today*, April, 32–35.
14 Scott, C., & Dinham, S. (2005). Parenting, teaching and self esteem. *The Australian Educational Leader, 27*(1), 28–30; Dinham, S., & Scott, C. (2007). Parenting, teaching and leadership styles. *The Australian Educational Leader, 29*(1), 30–32; 45.

5 | Teacher and school executive satisfaction, motivation and stress

Fate leads the willing, and drags along those who hang back.

(Seneca)

Introduction

Teachers and school executive staff are key drivers of educational achievement and their satisfaction and overall well-being is an important product of, and input to, school functioning.

An understanding of the sources of teachers' satisfaction, dissatisfaction and stress is necessary if we are to create and maintain convivial and productive teaching and learning environments.

This chapter considers the findings and implications arising from an international study of teacher satisfaction, motivation and health, the Teacher 2000 Project. This project built upon my earlier doctoral research into teacher resignation.[1]

Context of teacher satisfaction

One theme above all has resonated through education since the 1960s and that is change. Although there has always been pressure for schools to change, with growing change and complexity in society, change in education has become a constant, and shows no signs of easing, with greater intervention, scrutiny, accountability and pressure for improvement in all areas of education. This is part of an international phenomenon.

Change is of course, a natural part of life and there is no reason why educational employees, institutions or systems should be immune to or protected from change. However, what is problematic about change in education are the often conflicting motives and pressures for change and the various outcomes of attempts to facilitate change, outcomes that are not always perceived as positive for students and teachers.*

One of the many paradoxes about change in education is the pressure for schools to take on more and more social responsibilities (the 'extras'), with commensurate calls for greater attention to measurable outcomes in areas such as literacy and numeracy (the 'basics'). A further paradox is that while schools and teachers are being entrusted with more and more responsibility, the status of teachers has probably never been lower – 'we entrust you with more, we trust you less' – with frequent criticism directed against teachers and schools, especially government schools.

Another feature of change in education is the degree to which the pendulum swings. In many cases, what has been advocated and even mandated at one time has been reversed later, examples being school-based curriculum development versus central prescription and control over curricula, school self-management versus centralised administrative control of educational systems, and external examinations versus internal assessment. Even the prime function of school leaders has swung from administration, to management, to educational leadership.[2]

Additionally, where devolution of responsibility to schools has occurred, many would argue that this has proven to be a new form of centralisation and control, with greater accountability and scrutiny accompanying this greater 'autonomy'.

Changing education must inevitably mean changing teachers, or at least more pressure being placed on teachers to change both themselves and their practices. As Andy Hargreaves has noted, rather than achieving 'educational ends', these changes have in many cases been promulgated in order to facilitate both 'economic regeneration' and the 'rebuilding of national cultures and identities', such attempts occurring within a context of greater criticism of education and tighter economic constraints. Hargreaves has noted the 'twin realities of change' as being 'ideological compliance' and 'financial self-reliance'.[3] A third reality, in many cases, is undoubtedly greater workloads to meet the demands of change and, in some cases, resultant 'change fatigue', dissatisfaction and stress.

When considering the effects of teaching on teachers, a vast, often vaguely defined and overlapping literature on such matters as teacher status, teacher stress, teacher burn-out, teacher morale, teacher satisfaction and teacher motivation is encountered, a literature that has expanded

---

*   In this chapter, the term 'teacher' is used generically to encompass principals, others holding formal promotions positions in schools, classroom teachers, relief/casual teachers and specialist teaching staff such as school counsellors and librarians.

commensurate with educational innovation and change in the period since the 1960s.

Frequently, these matters are also the subject of debate and discussion in the public arena, the media, in election campaigns, and in teachers' salary disputes.

The Teacher 2000 Project
Earlier studies

In the early 1990s I undertook doctoral research which grew out of my previous studies and interest in organisational behaviour. My PhD study was essentially qualitative and involved interviewing 57 teachers, school executive and system officials who had resigned from one educational system over a 12-month period. I was interested in issues such as why these people had entered teaching, their views on their training, their early experiences of teaching, the things that they found most satisfying and most dissatisfying in their teaching career, the background to and reasons for their resignation and their current employment.[4]

Following the teacher resignation study, I undertook another interview-based qualitative study, this time with the partners of teachers (coincidentally, also 57 participants but not connected with the earlier sample).[5] Many of those interviewed in the previous study had spoken of the pressures of teaching and how these spilled over to family life because of the 'open-endedness' of teaching and teachers' inability to 'switch off'. I was interested in exploring further how teaching affects teachers and their families and the coping strategies they employed. I had also been involved in a national study of teacher induction.[6] In yet another study, I had used my background in human geography to conduct an analysis of Australia's ageing teaching population and its implications.[7] All these studies provided useful background to the Teacher 2000 Project.

My doctoral study involving teachers and executive who had resigned revealed that the factors contributing to teacher satisfaction were largely discrete from those contributing to teacher dissatisfaction (i.e. a 'two-factor' model consistent with the influential work of Herzberg from the 1950s[8]), and that when teachers made the decision to resign, the sources and strength of their 'satisfiers' were basically unchanged, while it was the increase in the strength of their 'dissatisfiers' that had tipped the balance and precipitated the decision to resign.

Overwhelmingly, satisfiers were phenomena and rewards intrinsic to teaching; that is, 'core business', including student achievement, teacher accomplishment, changing student attitudes and behaviours in a positive way, recognition from others, efficacy and self-growth, and positive relationships with students, staff and others. Satisfiers were largely universal across sex, teaching experience, position held, location and type of school.

Dissatisfiers, on the other hand, were phenomena more extrinsic to the teaching of students, and included impacts of changes to educational policies and procedures, greater expectations on schools to deal with and solve social problems, the declining status of teachers in society coupled with increased criticism, poor-quality supervision, being treated impersonally by employers, new responsibilities for schools and increased administrative workloads. In short, dissatisfiers were phenomena perceived as detracting from or militating against the 'core business' of teaching students.

It was found that the relative strength of respondents' dissatisfiers had increased over time due to social and educational change, and that 'control' was a key issue, in that in many cases, imposed changes impacting on schools had to be implemented with little room for discretion on the part of principals and teachers and with little practical help from above, with resultant dissatisfaction. A direct causal link was established between participants' increased dissatisfaction and increased stress, with lack of control over workload a key influence.

In summary, teachers who had resigned maintained that they still found the core business of teaching to be highly satisfying at the time they resigned. It was increased dissatisfaction and in some cases stress that was mainly responsible for their resignation.

Following these earlier studies, Catherine Scott and I began planning a survey-based study to test some of these emergent findings. Building on the qualitative studies, the intention was to survey a relatively large number of teachers and school executive to increase understanding in the area and to, in turn, better inform decision making and policy formation in the areas of teacher satisfaction, motivation and health. Full details of the methodology are available elsewhere, but to date, the instrument we developed from the earlier studies, coupled with two other standard instruments designed to measure commitment values (Novacek and Lazarus' 40-item version commitments scales) and mental health (the 12-item General Health Questionnaire), has been used with samples of teachers in Australia, New Zealand, England, the United States of America, Canada, Malta, Cyprus and several other sites, including most recently in Africa.[9]

The discussion that follows mainly refers to the following samples:

- 892 teachers and school executive from a representative sample of 71 government primary and secondary schools from across the greater Sydney region in NSW, Australia

- 609 teachers from 114 schools across England
- 600 teachers from schools in New Zealand.

Motivation to enter teaching

Motivation to be a teacher was measured in two ways. First, participants were invited to agree or disagree that seven *orientation to teaching* and two *preparedness to teach* items were true of them at the time they commenced their careers. Second, participants completed the modified version of the Novacek and Lazarus commitments scales.[10]

Table 5.1 contains the percentages of teachers from each country who agreed with the nine orientation to teaching/preparedness to teach items. Across the three countries, patterns of motivations for entering teaching were very similar.

In all three countries 'always wanting' to be a teacher was the most frequently endorsed reason for entering the profession. Responses for males and females were similar within each of the samples, although females were more likely to report that they had always wanted to be a teacher and that they thought teaching would fit in well with family commitments, while males were more likely to report that teaching was not their first choice of career and that they became a teacher because of a lack of other options.

Table 5.1 Orientation to teaching

Australia % True	England % True	New Zealand % True	
49	45	46	I always wanted to become a teacher.
40	40	43	Teaching was not my first choice of career.
20	18	24	I became a teacher because of a lack of other options.
13	6	10	There was pressure from my family to become a teacher.
34	31	32	I was attracted to teaching because of the hours and holidays.
44	32	40	I thought that teaching would fit in well with family commitments.
10	7	6	I was attracted to teaching because of the salary.
54	65	60	I had a realistic view of teaching before I began my training.
38	39	44	My training adequately prepared me for teaching.

Table 5.2 reports the sample means for the six commitments scales (each item was rated from 1 (Not at all important) to 7 (Extremely important).[11] Results were similar again for each of the three countries: *affiliation* is the most strongly endorsed personal commitment, followed closely by *altruism* and then *personal growth* values. The commitment that received the lowest endorsement in all three countries was the need for *power and achievement*. These results would indicate that teachers surveyed were in the job for the 'right reasons'; that is, valuing working with others, wanting to help others and desiring personal growth and efficacy.

Table 5.2 Commitments (Novacek and Lazarus' commitments scales)

	Australia	England	New Zealand
Scale		Means	
Affiliation	5.53	5.46	5.54
Altruism	5.39	5.34	5.44
Personal growth	5.38	5.39	5.48
Stress avoidance	5.14	5.15	5.03
Sensation seeking	5.12	5.11	5.24
Power and achievement	4.93	4.94	4.90

1 = Not at all important, 7 = Extremely important

Aspects of their work teachers and school executive find most satisfying

During the Australian phase of the research, data reduction was performed on the 75 satisfaction items (derived from my doctoral findings) with the aim of exploring the structure of satisfaction/dissatisfaction and developing a series of scales to measure these. Factor analyses and further model-building resulted in the development of a 10-factor model of teacher satisfaction.[12]

The 10 factors derived from the 75 items rated by participants were named as follows (highest loading item included in brackets). Table 5.3 presents the mean scores for each of the 10 scales.

1 *School leadership, climate, decision making* (item with the highest loading 'your satisfaction with leadership in your school')
2 *Promotion procedures and opportunities* ('… current criteria for promotion')
3 *School infrastructure* ('… your school's material resources')

4. *School reputation* ('... pupil behaviour in your school')
5. *Status and image of teachers* ('... status of teachers in society')
6. *Student achievement* ('... your capacity to influence student achievement')
7. *Pastoral care* ('... your capacity to change student behaviour')
8. *Workload* ('... your current workload overall')
9. *Change and change management* ('... degree of support to implement change')
10. *Professional self-growth* ('... your acquisition/development of professional skills').

Table 5.3 Mean scores for satisfaction scales

Scale	Australia	England	New Zealand
		Means	
Student achievement	5.36	5.53	5.45
Self-growth	5.31	5.22	5.31
Pastoral care	4.78	4.99	5.02
School leadership	4.37	4.25	4.63
School reputation	4.31	4.55	4.68
School infrastructure	3.69	3.44	4.07
Workload	3.46	2.80	3.44
Promotion	3.09	3.64	4.29
Change/Change management	2.68	2.80	3.34
Status	2.18	2.34	2.76

1 = High dissatisfaction, 4 = Neutral, 7 = High satisfaction

Once again, there are strong similarities in the findings. Broadly consistent with the results for the commitments scales, teachers in all three countries reported highest satisfaction with items and scales concerned with their 'core business'. This 'first domain' covered the areas of facilitating student achievement, their own growth, and pastoral care aspects of teaching such as working with students and assisting them to become better people.

Teachers and school executive across the three samples were dissatisfied with aspects of teaching outside their control, such as those associated with imposed workload, change and change management, and promotion opportunities and procedures. They were most dissatisfied with aspects of their standing in society such as their status, perceptions of this work (open-ended comments mentioned 'long holidays', 'short days', 'women's work', 'not a real job') and criticism from the media, employer, politicians and community generally.

However, the study also revealed a 'third domain' of teacher satisfaction. While teachers reported high satisfaction with their 'core business' and were simultaneously highly dissatisfied with matters in the broader community and profession over which they had little control, there was also a 'third domain' of occupational satisfaction revealed by the research findings. School-based factors outside the classroom, such as items to do with school leadership, school reputation and school infrastructure, were rated as neither highly satisfying nor highly dissatisfying overall, and it was here that most variation from school to school occurred, with school leadership the most important influence on participants' reported satisfaction with school-based items.

Participants were also asked to rate their overall satisfaction with teaching on a seven-point scale. Because of the multi-dimensional nature of occupational satisfaction noted above, single or global measures of satisfaction have been found to be unreliable, and so it was in this case. In all three countries, mean satisfaction scores for participants were around the 'neutral' level, or about 4, the mid-point on the 1–7 scale.

However, when distributions of scores were considered it was found that results for this item were bi-modal; participants tended to be polarised at opposite ends of the scale, with few people in the middle. The implication of this finding is that there are two broad groups of teachers in many schools: those who are satisfied overall and those who are not. There is not a normal curve – few teachers are actually 'sitting on the fence' – and is something for school leaders to think about.

The findings for changed satisfaction were also interesting, with participants reporting an overall fall in satisfaction with teaching since commencing their careers. This is counter to the evidence derived from earlier work, that employees generally report a rise in satisfaction over time due to growing self-efficacy, promotion, higher salary, greater responsibility and recognition. This situation is also helped by the fact that some of those who don't like the work or who don't experience professional growth resign. This was not the case with this study and was explained by the growing influence of school-based, and especially societal and systemically based factors, which were found to have eroded participants' overall satisfaction with teaching.

Another interesting finding was that it was not age or years of experience that predicted overall reported satisfaction or changed satisfaction, but time in current school and current position. In other words, based on these findings, being too long in one school or in a position within that school, predicts lower satisfaction and a greater fall in satisfaction. This was supported by the findings for the General Health Questionnaire (GHQ) reported later and is also something to think about in the current situation of an ageing teaching workforce, many of whom have been in one school for many years. This finding reinforced some of the findings from the earlier interview-based studies, where teachers had admitted that a change in school would be good for them, and presumably their students, but that they were reluctant to change schools. The usual reason given, aside from financial cost, was that these teachers feared having to re-establish their 'discipline' and reputation in a new school. The challenge, then, is to reinvigorate teachers who have been too long in the same environment. Obviously this is a general finding and there would be exceptions. Some long-serving teachers are the 'rocks' on which a school is built, as evident in the HSC study.[13]

Overall, for the samples of teachers in all three countries, satisfaction (or not) with their current workload was the strongest predictor of overall satisfaction and change in satisfaction. Teachers in England were marginally the least satisfied overall, with both open-ended and quantitative data pointing to factors such as public criticism of teachers and schools, the demands of the national curriculum, and the pressures of Ofsted (Office for Standards in Education, now called Office for Standards in Education, Children's Services and Skills) 'inspections' being cited as powerful negative influences. Teachers in New Zealand were marginally more satisfied overall than teachers in Australia, who were in turn more satisfied than the teachers surveyed in England.

These three studies and the later replications in other countries have confirmed the important influence of the extant educational climate and context on teacher satisfaction within individual schools and systems.

Table 5.4 Overall satisfaction and change in satisfaction since commencing teaching

Scale	Australia	England	New Zealand
Overall satisfaction	4.07	3.92	4.25
1 = Highly dissatisfied, 4 = Neutral, 7 = Highly satisfied			
Change in satisfaction	3.41	3.23	3.66
1 = Now more highly dissatisfied, 4 = No change, 7 = Now more highly satisfied			

Mental stress

The score on the 12-item version of the General Health Questionnaire (GHQ) was calculated as an item average with higher scores indicating higher levels of distress.

Expressed as such, scores of 1.00 to 2.00 represent well-being, between 2.00 and 3.00 increasing levels of distress, and over 3.00, high levels of distress. The samples displayed, on average, a reasonable degree of mental well-being, although once again, the teachers in England were the 'unhappiest'. However, in all three countries there were significant numbers of teachers recording high levels of distress; that is, with reported mean scores over 3.00.

Table 5.5 General Health Questionnaire results

	Item mean scores
Australia	2.11
New Zealand	2.11
England	2.18

Influence of position

The various satisfaction scales and the GHQ revealed a further interesting finding: international research had demonstrated a relationship between physical health and occupational status/level of appointment; that is, people who hold higher level positions in organisations enjoy better physical health on average than those in lower positions.

Researchers have speculated that this may be in part due to the fact that individuals occupying lower positions have less control or discretion over the pace and allocation of their work than those occupying higher positions in the workplace. Poorer physical health is thus mediated by lower levels of mental well-being.[14]

Internationally, many of those working in school education have experienced 'control' being taken from them by rapid and constant educational change imposed from 'outside' and 'above', as education has become increasingly politicised and open to external scrutiny and involvement by various stakeholders. The pace and extent of this change has varied across nations and it can be predicted that its effects will also vary according to its intensity and scope. (This was confirmed when comparing the findings for Australia, England and New Zealand, with those from later replications of the Teacher 2000 Project in countries such as Malta and Cyprus, countries which have experienced less educational change and where teacher status and reported satisfaction have remained high.)

The GHQ findings indicated that those holding higher positions in the Australian sample (principals, deputies) tended to report better levels of mental health than those in lower positions. However, those holding 'middle management' executive positions (secondary heads of department, primary lower executive) tended to score below classroom teachers on the GHQ, counter to the situation reported with prior research where classroom teachers would have been expected to report the lowest scores. (In England and New Zealand neither position nor type of school predicted the GHQ of an individual to the extent it did with the Australian sample.[15])

Those in middle management positions such as department heads in secondary schools and executive teachers below the rank of deputy principal in primary schools occupy crucial 'linking' positions. They have high teaching loads, with responsibilities above and below them, and report feeling 'squeezed' and compromised by the interpersonal and administrative demands of the role for which they feel they were largely unprepared. A later study I conducted with four doctoral students explored this phenomenon in more detail and found that role overload, role conflict and role ambiguity were important factors in the stress and dissatisfaction experienced by middle managers (in this case, secondary heads of department) in schools.[16]

With the Australian sample, those who scored worst of all on the GHQ and the various satisfaction scales were Advanced Skills Teachers, a position introduced in many Australian jurisdictions to recognise and reward the classroom teacher who stays in the classroom. This initiative was largely a failure and the AST position has been removed or replaced in most systems.[17] In their open-ended comments, ASTs reported their dissatisfaction with the following: the additional responsibilities associated with their position, which they felt detracted from their teaching and for which they felt unprepared; being treated as 'wastepaper baskets' for roles others in the school were not prepared to take on, and the poor financial rewards that went with the position.

Once again, teachers in England scored most poorly on the GHQ, as they had on most of the other measures, reflecting the difficult context of education in that country at the time of the study.[18]

Implications of the teacher satisfaction research

The teacher satisfaction research clearly showed that teachers want to teach and school leaders want to support teaching and learning. However, attempts in recent times to make schools responsible for a raft of what were formerly community and family roles, to introduce more and more into school curricula to meet a range of disparate needs and agendas, to make schools more accountable for funding and to 'do more with less', to try to lift school performance through measuring and publicising student and school achievement, to criticise teachers and schools for being 'out of touch' with society, when every day they deal with it first hand through contact with its children – all these factors and more have been found to drive teacher status and satisfaction down and have made teaching a less attractive career for both practising and prospective teachers.

There are a number of imperatives arising from these findings. Teachers and schools cannot reasonably be expected to solve problems over which they have little control nor capacity to deal with. Educational systems, governments and society need to acknowledge their collective responsibility for the current extrinsic factors giving rise to worrying levels of teacher dissatisfaction and the erosion of teachers' intrinsic satisfaction. The increasing pace and scope of educational change has exacerbated this problem, rather than solving it, although clearly change is needed in many instances. It is clear that in some schools, continual pressure for change seems to have induced a 'victim', reactive, disempowered mentality, hindering school-based change and discouraging initiative.

While it is encouraging to find that leadership can make a difference to teacher and executive satisfaction at the school level, school leaders and teachers are largely at the mercy of a generally unsympathetic, increasingly demanding set of external forces, and need understanding, support and assistance to deal with this situation, rather than criticism and blame for failure to deliver what society is demanding of them.

However, while it is understandable that this disempowering context might result in a loss of momentum, and even a defensive stance, teachers, schools, teachers' unions, professional associations and others with an interest in education, need to take action to move into and engage with this somewhat hostile and critical 'outer domain' in order to play an active part in the current discourse on education and to help shape its future. Silence or blanket resistance in this instance will be interpreted as confirmation of society's criticisms and misconceptions of education and teachers.

Teachers need to ensure that the barricades do not go up around them in a futile and counter-productive attempt to keep these outer forces at bay. Instead, they need to adopt an attitude of openness – both to the community and to new ideas – to facilitate increased community appreciation of the many good things they do and to remedy the damaging misconceptions much of the community has about schools today. The leaders of the schools in the AESOP study showed how this can be done.

There also needs to be an audit of current teacher and school executive responsibilities and a reconceptualisation of teachers' work to enable them to concentrate more on their core business which they find so satisfying. This will require others such as administrative and specialist staff – both teaching and non-teaching – to assume some of the responsibilities and roles currently being shifted to teachers and schools. This will also require teachers to let go some of their current tasks, something which primary teachers in particular are strangely reluctant to do, despite complaining about being overloaded.[19]

In the case of primary teaching, I think we have reached the stage where a degree of teacher specialisation is needed. An increasingly crowded primary school curriculum means generalist teachers often have a breadth but not a depth of knowledge.[20] (See *The case for subject specialisation in primary teaching* at the end of this chapter.)

Looming teacher shortages in many countries makes the reconceptualisation of teachers' work even more urgent, and may indirectly lead to a greater regard for teachers, as we tend not to recognise the value of anything until it is absent or in short supply. Something which militates against higher teacher status is the mass nature of the profession.

Authentic productive partnerships based upon mutual respect and understanding are needed to move education forward, and outward. As Andy Hargreaves and Michael Fullan have noted:

> *It is not only up to teachers and administrators to figure out and work for what they hope for: it is up to parents, students, policy makers, labour and business leaders, politicians and the media as well. Rebuilding and redefining education, and its relationship to the world 'out there', in other words, is a job for citizens and society as a whole.*[21]

Teachers and schools thus need to build bridges with those occupying the outer domain, not walls, and to mobilise those reservoirs of goodwill and support that do exist. Once again, the leaders in the AESOP study demonstrated an awareness of the importance of looking outwards, building relationships and the rewards that this can bring.

Strategies to enhance teacher satisfaction

For those interested in facilitating teacher satisfaction and in reducing dissatisfaction and stress, the following suggestions arising from my earlier doctoral work, the Teacher 2000 Project, and later studies might be helpful. Full details and explanations are provided elsewhere[22] and are implicit in some of the earlier discussions. These areas are important and tend to be overlooked in the day-to-day 'hurly burly' of school life, although as we have seen, the 'best' teachers and leaders give these areas high priority regardless.

In advocating the following strategies, I need to issue my usual warning that these are not 'quick fixes'. I suggest you use these as a framework for reflection, planning and action but that you also need to carefully consider the context of your school – the history, staff, students, parents and community and what you are trying to achieve. I have not included actions that need to be taken by educational systems, which also have responsibilities in the areas of teacher recognition and satisfaction.

How to facilitate enhanced teacher satisfaction and reduce dissatisfaction:

1. Continually maintain and seek to improve the physical environment of the school and teachers' workspaces.
2. Create a climate where genuine recognition is freely given and achievement is celebrated.
3. Be clear on your expectations for yourself and others and apply standards fairly and consistently, while demonstrating compassion and flexibility when needed.
4. Drive out negativity and the 'victim' mentality; set a positive example.
5. Strive for the 'personal touch' in professional interactions and seek to develop mutual respect and trust.
6. Make social interaction and conviviality a high priority; people should enjoy coming to work.
7. Publicise student, teacher and school achievement frequently and in varied ways; you can talk up the school, talk it down, or say nothing – the choice is yours.
8. Facilitate effective two-way horizontal and vertical communication and reduce barriers between departments and groups of staff.
9. The 'invisible' principal or leader? – get out and about, take a personal interest in teachers, other staff and students, and be available when needed.
10. Build productive external partnerships; bridges are better than walls.
11. Facilitate real, representative community involvement; take the school to the community; focus on improving school–community communications and relations.
12. Provide opportunities for teacher rejuvenation, especially for long-term staff at the school.
13. Seek opportunities for 'new blood' to enter the school.
14. Reassess the workloads of 'middle managers' – they are crucial and need support.
15. Find ways to let all staff focus on their 'core business' as much as possible.
16. Provide supportive rather than judgemental supervision but don't shy away from tough decisions and confronting people when necessary.

17 Assist teachers to identify their professional needs and to act to meet these; invest in teacher learning; model learning.
18 Provide staff with prompt, constructive feedback, both 'good' and 'bad'.
19 Provide staff with the means of giving you feedback and be seen to act on this; conduct exit interviews or surveys with staff who leave the school/teaching.
20 Aspire to the highest professional standards and expect professionalism in return; strive to be an authoritative leader and to demonstrate moral authority.

The appendix that follows is something of a personal 'hobby-horse'. There is already quite a deal of ad hoc subject specialisation in primary schools and I think we need to formalise this, particularly in the cases of mathematics, science and ICT, coupled with a greater focus on literacy.

Chapter 6 then considers the important issue of teachers' professional learning.

Acknowledgements

Once again I need to recognise the contribution made by Catherine Scott to the work highlighted in this chapter. Catherine was mainly responsible for the statistical design and data analysis for the Teacher 2000 Project; co-directed the Australian and international studies with me; directed the English replication, and advised the international teams conducting subsequent replications on data analysis.

The case for subject specialisation in primary teaching[23]

In 2002–03, the Australian Government conducted a Review of Teaching and Teacher Education, one of many over recent decades.[24] The review committee was asked to report on issues of teacher supply and demand, the current level of teacher skills, and the effectiveness of pre-service and in-service education and training for teachers. The aim of the review was to 'help build a culture of lifelong learning and innovation in Australia's schools'.

I was a member of that review committee and during the review and through my research, professional development work with teachers and visits to schools, I became convinced that Australian education had reached the point where the expectations being placed on primary teachers to teach all areas of the curriculum, as well as addressing all the other societal issues being shifted to schools, had become unreasonable, if not untenable.

It is clear that many current concerns, such as secondary student achievement, post-compulsory retention and attracting suitable people to university courses for careers in maths and science, have their origins in the quality of teaching our young people receive in primary schooling.

As the primary school curriculum has become increasingly crowded with social 'extras', accompanied by greater standardised testing and reporting of the 'basics', it has become more difficult to train, professionally develop and support primary teachers. As the breadth of teaching increases, inevitably, the depth and effectiveness decreases. It has thus become even harder to prepare beginning teachers.

For a variety of reasons, we have seen a general drift away from the study of curriculum or subject areas since teacher education moved into universities in the late 1980s. Over the same three decades, teacher education programs have become longer, particularly in primary education, where four years of pre-service undergraduate training is now standard. For graduate entry, two years of teacher education is increasingly the norm. Theoretically, longer periods of pre-service education should better equip our teachers for the realities of teaching, yet this is not necessarily so.

The longer time available for pre-service education has been soaked up by increasing demands and often competing ideologies. Many areas, views and subjects jostle for inclusion. Some are mandated by various stakeholders and education ministers, including Indigenous education, English as a Second Language, languages, Information and Communication Technology, special education, behaviour management, and so on. All are worthy and have their supporters, but each adds to the pressure on university courses, teaching staff and resources. Compromises are inevitable and can lead to conflict over what to omit or reduce in priority.

In these academic and ideological turf wars, 'traditional' curriculum areas have tended to lose out to areas seen as more important and relevant in this postmodernist, poststructuralist era, such as subjects about diversity – the icing has replaced the cake, the seasoning has replaced the main course. The view from some is that curriculum areas can and should be integrated; that process is more important than content; that student-centred activity is better than teacher direction; and that studying the 'nuts and bolts' of school curricula and assessment is somehow wrong in the current context.

Subject content knowledge has been portrayed by some as rote learning and recitation of facts, names, dates and places, and is seen as less worthy than critical thinking and the acknowledgement of multiple social realities. Learning to learn is seen as preferable to learning. Teacher-directed learning is seen as old-fashioned, even harmful, while student activity and choice is championed, regardless of what that activity or choice might entail.

Based on my research and experience, beginning teachers have two fundamental needs. They want to know what to teach, and how to teach it. Everything else should support these ends. Many studies of quality or effective teaching have demonstrated the need for teachers to have strong, deep subject matter knowledge, as detailed in earlier chapters. The backbone of any teacher education program must be the school curriculum, something with which all practising teachers must engage.

For effective and powerful teaching and learning to occur in the primary years, I believe we have reached the point where a degree of subject specialisation needs to be introduced to primary teacher training and teaching. Whenever I mention this, the usual reaction is shock and horror that primary schools could adopt the perceived worst aspects of high schools – multiple teachers, teaching subjects rather than students and the 'tyranny of the bells'. After all, one of the principles of middle schooling is to ease the primary–secondary transition through making the middle years more like primary schooling and less like secondary schooling. My heretical view is that there are actually advantages in making the primary years more like secondary education. This too could make the upper primary–secondary transition less problematic.

In my experience, high schools today are more orderly than primary schools. The primary school day is fragmented with numerous disruptions and changes of activity and these are more intrusive than in the typical high school. It is difficult to finish anything and primary teachers struggle to master and cover all aspects of the curriculum. Science is particularly problematic, as recent reviews have demonstrated. Many teachers admit they lack the knowledge and expertise to teach science effectively and thus it receives less attention and treatment in the typical school day than it should.

We will continue to need the generalist primary teacher, but I believe that two broad teaching specialisations would attract suitably talented people to teaching – including some presently deterred by the breadth of the primary curriculum – and enable greater depth in teacher education, teaching, and teacher professional learning. It might also help to attract more men to primary teaching, although the quality of a teacher is more important than that teacher's personal qualities.

One primary teaching specialisation could encompass maths, science and technology, with a strong emphasis on numeracy, while the other could address the humanities, with a strong emphasis on literacy. Some areas of the curriculum such as physical education would be common to each. All teachers would still be teachers of literacy and numeracy as well as performing the usual pastoral care, organisational and extra-curricular roles. Over time, additional specialisations could be added, again in areas where teachers report they are inadequately prepared, such as languages.

As these specialist teachers enter teaching, they will in turn enable other generalist teachers to specialise through being released from some of their present, subject-based responsibilities. They could also be supported through team-teaching with these subject specialists. I suspect primary students would actually welcome the variety and challenge resulting from greater teacher specialisation.

Under this proposal, a pre-service primary teacher could do the following: undertake a degree in the relevant subject areas, then complete a one- or two-year end-on teacher training program; undertake a four-year education degree designed to address their specialisation, or complete a suitable concurrent double degree in, say, science and education. Mature entrants with relevant industry experience might also be attracted from outside teaching to such specialist roles.

The time saved in primary teacher training from not having to address all areas of the curriculum would enable greater depth of treatment and understanding of both subject knowledge and teaching methods, as well as providing for more time in schools and other settings depending on the model adopted. Professional experience could also be more focused.

Some of these teachers could undertake a qualification to enable them to teach in the first two years of high school to facilitate middle schooling initiatives.

Under such an arrangement, primary school students (and teachers) would have the benefit of working with someone with a greater depth of knowledge, and hopefully passion for their specialisation, which would provide a firmer foundation for student success in the primary years of schooling and beyond.

It is time we looked seriously at the potential benefits of introducing a limited amount of formal specialisation to primary teaching, over and above that which currently occurs on a loose, school-by-school basis.

This needs to take place within the context of a broader discussion on the overall purposes of primary and secondary schooling, which might result in the greater use of para-professionals and support staff in schools so that teachers can concentrate on a more limited range of professional responsibilities. Such specialisation would also complement and strengthen any moves to narrow and deepen the primary school curriculum.

Notes

1. Dinham, S. (1992). *Human perspectives on the resignation of teachers from the New South Wales Department of school education: Towards a model of teacher persistence*. Doctor of Philosophy thesis, University of New England, Armidale; Dinham, S. (1993). Teachers under stress. *Australian Educational Researcher*, 20(3), December, 1–16; Dinham, S. (1995). Time to focus on teacher satisfaction, *Unicorn*, 21(3), 64–75.
2. Dinham, S. (2007). The waves of leadership, *The Australian Educational Leader*, 29(3), 20–21, 27.
3. Hargreaves, A. (1994). *Changing teachers, changing times*. London: Cassell, p. 5.
4. Dinham (1992); Dinham (1993); Dinham (1995).
5. Dinham, S. (1997). Teaching and teachers' families. *Australian Educational Researcher, AARE*, August, 24(2), 59–88.
6. Dinham, S. (1992). Teacher induction: Implications for administrators. *The Practising Administrator*, 14(4), 30–33; Baumgart, N., Dinham, S., Khamis, M., & NSW DSE. (1992). *Review of Australian Teacher Induction*. Sydney: NSW DSE.
7. Dinham, S. (1996). In loco grandparentis?: The challenge of Australia's ageing teacher population. *International Studies in Educational Administration*, 24(1), 16–30.
8. Herzberg, F., Mausner, B., & Snyderman, B. (1959). *The motivation to work*. NY: John Wiley & Sons.
9. There have been many publications and conference papers arising from these series of replications. Key publications include: Dinham, S., & Scott, C. (1996). *The Teacher 2000 Project: A study of teacher satisfaction, motivation and health*. Penrith: University of Western Sydney, Nepean; Dinham, S., & Scott, C. (1997). The advanced skills teacher: An opportunity missed? *Unicorn*, 23(3), 36–49; Dinham, S., & Scott, C. (1998). A three domain model of teacher and school executive satisfaction. *Journal of Educational Administration*, 36(4), 362–378; Scott, C., Cox, S., & Dinham, S. (1999). The occupational motivation, satisfaction and health of English school teachers. *Educational Psychology*, 19(3), 287–308; Dinham, S., & Scott, C. (2000). Moving into the third, outer domain of teacher satisfaction. *Journal of Educational Administration*, 38(4), 379–396; Scott, C.,

Stone, B., & Dinham, S. (2001). I love teaching but ..., International patterns of teacher discontent. *Education Policy Analysis Archives, 9*(28), 1–7; Dinham, S., & Scott, C. (2002). Pressure points: School executive and educational change. *Journal of Educational Enquiry, 3*(2), 35–52. Scott, C., & Dinham, S. (2002) The beatings will continue until quality improves: Carrots and sticks in the search for educational improvement. *Teacher Development, 6*(1), 15–31; Scott, C., & Dinham, S. (2003). The development of scales to measure teacher and school executive occupational satisfaction. *Journal of Educational Administration, 41*(1), 74–86.

10 Novacek, J., & Lazarus, R.S. (1990). The structure of personal commitments. *Journal of Personality* (Vol. 58, No. 4), 693–715.

11 See Dinham, S., & Scott, C. (2000). Moving into the third, outer domain of teacher satisfaction. *Journal of Educational Administration, 38*(4), 379–396 for more detailed findings, including standard deviations.

12 See Scott, C., & Dinham, S. (2003). The development of scales to measure teacher and school executive occupational satisfaction. *Journal of Educational Administration, 41*(1), 74–86.

13 For further exploration of this issue, see: Dinham, S., & Sawyer, W. (2004). Mobility and highly effective teachers: Re-visiting beliefs about 'over-stayers'. *Melbourne Studies in Education, 45*(2), 83–97.

14 See Marmot, M., Bosma, H., & Hemingway, H., et al. (1997). Contribution of job control and other risk factors to social variations in coronary heart disease incidence. *Lancet, 350,* 235–239.

15 For more detailed examination of these findings, see: Dinham, S., & Scott, C. (2002). Pressure points: School executive and educational change. *Journal of Educational Enquiry, 3*(2), 35–52.

16 Dinham, S., Brennan, K., Collier, J., Deece, A., & Mulford, D. (2000). The secondary head of department: Key link in the quality teaching and learning chain, *Quality Teaching Series.* No. 2, Australian College of Education, September, 1–35; Deece, A., Dinham, S., Brennan, K, Collier, J., & Mulford, D. (2003). The leadership capabilities and decision making of the secondary head of department. *Leading & Managing, 9*(1), 38–51; Collier, J., Dinham, S., Brennan, K., Deece, A., & Mulford, D. (2002). Perceptions and reality of the work of the secondary head of department. *International Studies in Educational Administration, 30*(2), 17–26.

17 For a detailed examination of the AST, see Dinham, S., & Scott, C. (1997). The advanced skills teacher: An opportunity missed? *Unicorn, November, 23*(3), 36–49.

18 See Scott, C., Cox, S., & Dinham, S. (1999). The occupational motivation, satisfaction and health of English school teachers. *Educational Psychology, 19*(3), 287–308.

19 Dinham, S., & Scott, C. (1998). *Reconceptualising teachers' work*. Paper presented to the Australian College of Education, National Conference, Canberra, 28 September.

20 See Dinham, S. (2007). Overcrowding the curriculum – Still. *Directions in Education, 16*(15), 2–3; Dinham, S. (2007). Specialist primary teachers: Experts

in the field. ACER. Available at: http://www.acer.edu.au/documents/Dinham_SpecialistTeachers.pdf; Dinham, S. (2006) New formula needed to solve problems in schools. *Sydney Morning Herald*, 31 August, p. 13.
21 Hargreaves, A., & Fullan, M. (1998). *What's worth fighting for out there?* Mississauga, Ontario: Ontario Public School Teachers' Federation.
22 See Dinham, S. (1995). Time to focus on teacher satisfaction. *Unicorn, 21*(3), 64–75.
23 Dinham, S. (2007). *Specialist primary teachers: Experts in the field.* Melbourne: ACER. Available at: http://www.acer.edu.au/documents/Dinham_SpecialistTeachers.pdf
24 Committee for the Review of Teaching and Teacher Education. (2003). *Australia's teachers: Australia's future advancing innovation, science, technology and mathematics: Main report.* Canberra: DEST.

6 The importance of professional learning: Building a learning community

Knowledge is power.

(Francis Bacon)

Introduction

Teachers' professional learning has been shown to be central to successful teaching and effective schools.

This chapter reviews traditional and emerging approaches to teachers' professional learning before presenting a framework for developing and maintaining a learning community in education. This is derived from the research studies described to date and additional projects with which I have been involved. While none of the projects was about teachers' professional learning per se, each project added to an overall understanding of the role and nature of building learning communities for fostering quality teaching and student achievement.

Traditional and emerging approaches to teacher professional learning

Traditional approaches to teachers' professional learning tend to be linear, reflecting the broad stages of a teacher's career:

- formal pre-service teacher education
- on the job, ad hoc professional experience
- involvement with professional associations
- informal self-directed professional reading and learning
- formal in-service courses provided by employers (in school, out of school)
- formal postgraduate study
- other short courses

In Australia, the widespread provision of professional in-service learning for teachers really only dates back to the early 1970s, when Commonwealth funding for professional learning became available.

Table 6.1 below provides a general overview of the major characteristics of professional development for teachers in the 1970s, contrasted with current trends.

Table 6.1 Trends in teacher professional learning since the 1970s

From	To
Centralised	Decentralised professional learning
System responsibility	Individual, collective responsibility
Off the shelf	Tailored learning
Generalised	Contextualised
Off site, apart	On site, embedded
Inputs	Emphasis on outcomes
Passive	Interactive learning
External expert	External partners, advisers
Individual learning	Community learning
Theory based	Problem based
Transactional	Relational
Changing things	Changing people
Learning by seeing, hearing	Action learning
University degrees	Learning modules and short courses
Using research	Doing research
Paper based	Online learning
Broad focus	Student/learning focus

More recent approaches to teacher professional learning to augment these earlier approaches have included the following (running across these is greater use of online learning, including the use of learning 'blogs' and the development of online learning communities):

- action research
- action learning
- formal mentoring and coaching

- professional standards accreditation/certification (mandatory, voluntary)
- university accredited professional learning modules
- learning communities.

This chapter is mainly concerned with the concept of *building learning communities* and *action learning*, a particular type of learning which has been found to be very effective in the right circumstances (see *Action learning* at the end of this chapter).

Background: The individual teacher, school effectiveness and learning communities

Over many decades, films, books and television have portrayed the heroic, individual 'born' teacher battling against the odds to rein in unruly, uncaring students and fire within them a love of learning, often coming up against equally uncaring fellow teachers and inept principals in the process (see *To Sir with Love*, *Stand and Deliver*, *Dead Poets Society* and *Freedom Writers*, for examples of this genre). In the same schools where these teachers work their magic, students of other teachers are stultified and demoralised. Toole and Louis see this ongoing media fascination reinforcing an educational research tradition focusing on the attributes or traits of individual teachers.[1]

In her recent book *Powerful teacher education*, Linda Darling-Hammond describes the belief that 'good teachers are born and not made' as one of education's 'most damaging myths'; one that has gained the standing of a 'superstition', with harmful consequences for teacher education and schooling.[2] Obviously, if teachers are born and not made, there is no need for, or point to, teachers' professional learning. Research evidence, however, points conclusively to the fact that teaching is not a matter of innate qualities, but of learning and growth.[3]

This somewhat romantic, melodramatic view of teaching has persisted, while behind the scenes in education the attention of researchers turned as early as the mid-1960s to the issue of school effectiveness, as detailed in Chapter 1. The question of why some schools seemed to achieve superior results compared with other similar schools began to exercise minds. Up until this time, as we have noted previously, the prevailing view was that schools made no difference to children's development or achievement, which was largely pre-determined by heredity, family background and socio-economic context.[4]

The stages in school effectiveness research, initially centred in the United States of America, have been briefly described earlier. Reynolds et al. have synthesised these as:

1 *Input–output economic studies* (mid-1960s to early 1970s) which focused on the impact of human and physical resources upon outcomes
2 *Effective schools studies* (early to late 1970s) which focused on the addition of process variables and a wider range of school outcomes
3 *School improvement studies* (late 1970s to mid-1980s) incorporating school effectiveness correlates into schools through various programs
4 *Context variables* (late 1980s to present) introduced, coupled with more sophisticated methodologies.

There had been a related focus on the role that leadership can play in school effectiveness in terms of administration and management, and later its influence on student achievement, as we have seen in previous chapters. An early concentration on principal leadership has broadened to include other leaders such as deputy principals, faculty or department heads and teachers themselves. The focus of attention has thus moved from the leader to leadership, with the importance of delegation, trust and empowerment being increasingly recognised. There has been a realisation that leadership has both formal and distributed/distributive aspects, with every teacher a potential leader.[5]

Notwithstanding large-scale work on school effectiveness and educational leadership, the general and unassailable view now is that it is the classroom teacher who adds most to the learning equation, with the exception of that which each student 'brings to the table' (see Chapter 1).[6]

Thus, while there has been ongoing interest in effective schools and effective school leadership from the mid-1960s, since the late 1980s there has been major emphasis placed upon researching, understanding and facilitating quality teaching in schools, because of the growing recognition, supported by many empirical studies, that teachers make the major in-school difference to student achievement. At the same time, the notion of organisations as learning systems or communities has come to the fore,[7] along with related concepts such as lifelong learning, collaboration, partnerships, mentoring, synergies, change and renewal.

In reviewing these developments, Kilpatrick, Barrett and Jones proposed the following definition:

> Learning communities are made up of people who share a common purpose. They collaborate to draw on individual strengths, respect a variety of perspectives, and actively promote learning opportunities. The outcomes are the creation of a vibrant, synergistic environment, enhanced potential for all members, and the possibility that new knowledge will be created.[8]

In education, research into the performance of individual teachers has revealed the importance of learning communities in influencing individual teacher effectiveness. Building collaboration and community amongst teachers has been found to be effective both in promoting teacher professional development and enhancing educational outcomes for students.[9]

Voulalas and Sharpe noted that the concept of the school as a learning community, while almost universally accepted as desirable, is still vague and ambiguous, as is the case with the concept of learning communities more generally. This lack of clarity can make attempts to develop learning communities in education and elsewhere problematic. Following a review of the literature on school learning communities and interviews with principals, Voulalas and Sharpe found that:

> When all the definitions were pieced together the school as a learning community was perceived as a place where life-long learning takes place for all stakeholders for their own continuous growth and development, teachers act as exemplary learners, students are prepared adequately for the future, and mistakes become agents for further learning and improvement. Furthermore, it is a place where collaboration and mutual support is nurtured, clear shared visions for the future are built, and the physical environment contributes to learning.[10]

However, while we now have a workable understanding of what an educational learning community looks like, operationalising the concept can be challenging. A key weakness to date has been the failure to address the 'how' aspects of establishing and maintaining learning communities.

What follows is an attempt to address this weakness. The discussion draws upon a series of research studies that reveal aspects, conditions and dynamics of creating and maintaining learning communities in educational settings, so that individual teachers can be engaged in professional learning with their colleagues to improve both their practice and the achievement of their students.

Case studies of learning communities in practice

As I have recounted, over the past decade I have been involved in a range of research projects that have examined aspects of quality or successful teaching. Below is a brief examination of four of these studies, two of which have been described in earlier chapters, with particular reference to the notion of learning communities and how these may improve teacher learning and performance and student achievement. Once again, the interested reader is referred to the references cited at the end of this chapter for a full explanation of methodological matters and lengthier treatment of the studies.

The three broad areas of teacher learning identified in each of the studies were:

- *Subject content knowledge* (what subject content to teach)
- *Subject pedagogic knowledge* (how to teach particular subject content)
- *Subject course knowledge* (subject/course curriculum, assessment, examination knowledge).

Following these case studies, commonalities with respect to educational learning communities are outlined and implications and conclusions explored.

1 HSC teaching success

This study of successful senior secondary teaching has been described in Chapter 2.[11] Briefly, while the study focused on individual teachers, a key finding, apart from the commonalities in personal qualities, attributes and actions of these teachers, was the view they commonly expressed that their success and that of their students was attributable in large measure to their colleagues in faculties and teaching teams. This was more than just a case of false modesty and was confirmed by other data. Faculties and teams were found to have placed a major emphasis on collaborative learning.

2 AESOP

The findings from this study have been described in Chapter 3. In considering the factors responsible for faculties and teams being able to achieve exceptional educational outcomes with their students, teachers' collaborative approaches to professional learning were found to be important.

Faculty staff and cross-school team members were ongoing learners and demonstrated an interest in and passion for their area which was contagious. Faculty heads and teachers shared latest approaches and knowledge with each other and were often linked with external bodies such as professional associations and colleagues at other schools. Faculty responsibilities for professional learning were shared and teachers took the lead on learning about various issues.

3 Evaluation of the Australian Government Quality Teaching Program

In 2004–05, a team from the University of Technology Sydney (Peter Aubusson and Laurie Brady) and the University of Wollongong (Steve

Dinham) conducted an evaluation of an activity, entitled *Quality Teaching Action Learning* (QTAL) *in New South Wales* (NSW) *Public Schools*, on behalf of the NSW Department of Education and Training (DET).

QTAL projects took place in 2004–05 and were funded through the Australian Government Quality Teaching Program (AGQTP). The evaluation brief from the DET was to investigate conditions influencing teachers' implementation of an inquiry-based approach to action learning. The evaluation encompassed 50 individual projects involving 82 NSW public (government) primary and secondary schools that had successfully tendered for grants to investigate school-based and school-driven action learning research, utilising the framework of the NSW DET 'model of pedagogy'.[12]

Within the overarching QTAL activity, each school or group of schools had pursued an individual project (e.g. gifted and talented programs, literacy, quality teaching in science, etc.).

The evaluation took in all 50 Quality Teaching Action Learning projects involving the 82 schools, and nine projects were selected and researched as case studies by members of the evaluation team.[13]

The approach usually taken by schools was to use the funding provided under the AGQTP to release small teams from some of their teaching duties to enable them to work together on an approved Quality Teaching Action Learning project with the assistance of a designated university adviser. Teams were typically volunteers and comprised a mixture of classroom teachers and those in formal leadership positions, although in some cases principals had encouraged the membership of certain individuals.

The evaluation found that the QTAL projects undertaken by school teams as part of the AGQTP were very successful overall, both in promoting and utilising action learning and in achieving individual project aims.

It was found that being part of such teams led to the professional growth of those involved and this was manifested in increased leadership activity and influence in the school and sometimes beyond. Recognising individual teachers and empowering them to be involved within the project teams was an important symbolic and practical act of distributing leadership in the project schools, and the process of being involved in the projects facilitated further leadership capacity and potential.

Overall, the evaluation found that:

1 Successful projects were built upon a genuine, recognised need in the school.
2 Successful projects had clear, agreed, achievable and suitable goals.
3 Support from the principal (and other leaders) was essential.
4 A credible, suitable leader for the project was also vital.

5 Successful projects were characterised by effective teams and team building.
6 Schools found it difficult to start and to build momentum.
7 It is important to maintain communication with all school staff about the school's project and its progress.
8 Academic partners provided valuable conceptual and theoretical background and assisted with framing, implementing and evaluating project proposals.
9 Teacher release time was a major factor in project success.
10 Schools found the Quality Teaching model a useful conceptual tool and vocabulary for discussion about pedagogy.
11 The most successful schools considered long-term sustainability of the project from the start.
12 Distributive leadership was both a factor in the success and an outcome of action learning.[14]
13 While there were initial indications that programs were successful, evidence of enhanced student outcomes was lacking due to the time frame of the projects and the evaluation.
14 There was limited sharing of the successes of school-based initiatives with other schools.
15 Schools and individuals valued and benefited from the sharing conferences held during the project period where project teams from across the state came together to learn, share and report.

Research data (derived from teachers, school project reports and journals, university academic partners and the researchers' site visits) demonstrated that the school-based Quality Teaching Action Learning projects had stimulated and enhanced teacher professional learning in the schools concerned, and in some cases, beyond the schools immediately involved with the projects. The use of teams of interested and committed teachers was fundamental to this process.

Team members were encouraged, empowered and grew in the course of the action learning projects. Important factors in the operation of teams and their projects included the time, focus and support for professional learning, the teamwork and collaboration of team members, and the work of team leaders. The willingness of principals to share power and responsibility and to respect and foster the capacity of others was also crucial.

While the time frame for the QTAL projects was less than a year, there was sufficient evidence to suggest that distributive leadership has the capacity, when aligned with teacher learning, to foster the phenomenon of the learning community. In many of the schools, work had already been undertaken on the project issue or problem and sustainability of the projects was built in from the start to keep the learning process going beyond the project time frame.

4 NSW Quality Teaching Awards: learning communities and distributed leadership

The New South Wales (NSW) Minister for Education and Training Quality Teaching Awards (QTA) were instigated by the then NSW Minister for Education and Training in 2000 to recognise *and* research quality teaching in that state. Since its inception, the QTA has been developed and administered by the NSW Branch of the Australian College of Educators (ACE).[15] I chaired the NSW QTA from their inception in 2000 until mid-2007 when I left NSW to take up my present position.

The QTA is open to teachers from all sectors and levels of education in NSW and is built upon a set of agreed professional teaching standards.[16] The award process involves referees' reports, development of a professional learning portfolio, and site assessment visits conducted by two external 'experts' in the field where teaching is observed and structured interviews with key people take place (i.e. with the candidate, fellow teachers, senior staff, students, community members, etc.).

Between 2001 and 2007, 336 government and non-government teachers from early childhood, primary, secondary, TAFE and university education in NSW received Quality Teaching Awards, and the awards were to be presented once more in 2008 with up to 60 additional awardees. As part of the QTA agenda on researching quality teaching, a series of research projects have been conducted with QTA recipients.[17]

Despite the QTA being awarded for individual teaching excellence, as with the HSC study reported above, it became apparent from the portfolio assessment and site visit processes that in many cases there was a group of people within the particular organisation or workplace committed to enhancing teaching and learning; that is, the QTA recipient was not acting alone.

It was decided to conduct a pilot study at two university sites where a QTA recipient had been identified through the assessment process as being an important member of such a group. We were particularly interested in the ecology of learning communities – how and why learning communities arise and how they are sustained.

The method was for two researchers to visit each site to interview the QTA recipient and other key staff. Study questions included:

1 Why and how did discussion on quality teaching arise within the group?

2   What was the process? What people and factors influenced the process? What assisted and constrained the process?
3   What have been the outcomes of the process to date? What is the evidence for these outcomes?
4   How sustainable are the changes? How dependent is the process on one person?
5   Are there wider implications for quality teaching and teacher learning?
6   What role if any did the QTA play in the process?

Overall, the findings of the pilot study indicated that a concerted effort had been made to focus on quality teaching and learning in Australian higher education.

The study showed how leadership, direction and pressure for quality teaching were being exerted on four fronts:

1   By the Commonwealth (federal) Government in asserting the status of quality teaching and learning alongside that of research in university funding and in auditing or quality assurance arrangements such as AUQA (Australian Universities Quality Agency).
2   By the Carrick Institute for Learning and Teaching in Higher Education (since re-named the Australian Learning and Teaching Council) with its support for quality teaching, specifically in this study through its award programs as a means by which university teachers can demonstrate excellence in teaching and be recognised and rewarded for this.
3   Through universities placing greater emphasis on teaching and learning through formal structures and support, such as teaching and learning centres and staff development for teaching and learning; a greater emphasis on teaching capacity in appointment, tenure and promotion, and through utilising awards for quality teaching such as the Carrick awards and the NSW QTA to both encourage and demonstrate excellence in teaching in that university.
4   Through the distributive leadership exhibited by individuals and groups of educators within the university, such as the QTA recipients studied here.

In respect of the fourth point above, the study gave insights into the complexities and uncertainties of the change process as groups of like-minded people coalesce, collaborate and act around a quality teaching agenda. It also underscored the value of peer-assessed processes carried out in a voluntary way – as with the QTA process – that enabled collegial reflection on teaching practice.

While there were outside pressures and assistance to improve teaching and learning such as those outlined in 1–3 above, it was apparent that the two university groups concerned had taken charge of a quality teaching agenda within this context. Concern for students, passion for the particular discipline, and wanting to improve teaching and learning created the impetus for conversation, reflection, learning and change. Those involved had taken action, with participation being voluntary and based on perceived needs. Others in the organisation were being involved with and influenced by the quality teaching initiatives to varying degrees through a ripple or contagion effect.

On a cautionary note, the study suggested that there may be a point of disjunction between the leadership, pressure and support that is exhibited by the university in support of quality teaching – that is, 'top-down' pressure for change – and the on-the-ground, day-to-day distributive leadership that is exhibited by the academics themselves working with colleagues through conversations and work in small circles on matters important to them – that is, 'bottom-up' initiatives for change. The extent to which community learning and change around quality teaching can be stimulated, forced or mandated without such on-the-ground commitment and agreement is questionable, particularly in a large organisation like a university where pressure for change can be avoided or minimal, tokenistic compliance can occur.

In both QTA university case studies, the individual preparing for and receiving a QTA added value to the learning of the group concerned, and the QTA process became part of the conversation around quality teaching.

The award to one of their number of a QTA was seen as warranted by the rest of the group and a source of group recognition and pride. However, advancing quality teaching was not seen as being mainly about rewards or recognition. That said, it is an inescapable fact that awards for quality teaching are being seen and used increasingly by universities and governments as indicators of the quality of their teaching, with such successes communicated to the wider environment.

Drawing from the case studies: How does a learning community develop and sustain itself?

In considering the findings of the four studies, common key principles, conditions and dynamics were identified in respect of learning communities.

It should be noted that the issue of loose definition remains. It is apparent that organisations can act as learning communities at all levels from the organisation as an overall formal entity, to formal sub-groupings, to cross-functional groups down to smaller and less formal learning teams. This range of operation can make definition problematic, yet in no way diminishes the potential of the phenomenon.

For these reasons, the urge to provide yet another definition of the learning community, and the educational learning community specifically, has been resisted. I'll leave that to others.

What then can we conclude about learning communities from the various research studies? What works? To answer these questions, the following commonalities were identified from the studies.

Focus on teaching and learning

1 Learning communities have a focus on learning and a desire to learn about learning and teaching; there is use of pedagogic terminology, models and theory, coupled with a conscious effort to de-prioritise administration and management and prioritise learning within the group.
2 Members of learning communities see themselves and their students as going somewhere, with learning being an ongoing process; learning becomes contagious, with others catching the 'bug'.
3 Within the group there is recognition that it is necessary to change the way people think if there is to be change in how they act, and thus learning, reflection and questioning are important.
4 Members of the group are concerned with establishing and maintaining upward, continuous cycles of improvement; they are not satisfied with the status quo.

Individual and collective belief and support

5 Group members possess and demonstrate commitment and respect for their profession and discipline; they believe in, even love their area and communicate this to others.
6 Members of the group pay attention to social maintenance, trying to make their school, department, or faculty a 'good place';[18] members respect and care for each other and their students as people, and social and professional relationships are important to group performance.

Problem solving

7 There is an emphasis on problem- or issue-based learning and recognition of what is important, with dialogue around identified issues and potential solutions.
8 Experimentation, risk taking and innovation in teaching and learning are encouraged and are a feature of learning communities; there is questioning rather than acceptance of constraints or problems.
9 Teaching and learning are context and person specific, with efforts to contextualise and modify as necessary externally derived solutions or approaches.

10 There is ongoing reflection on and evaluation of existing and new measures within the learning community, coupled with data-informed decision making.

Internal expectations and accountability

11 The group creates a climate of high expectations and professionalism which members rise to, not wanting to let anyone down, least of all their students.
12 Members of the group empower each other to take the lead in learning, in turn enhancing individual and group leadership capacity and effectiveness.
13 Accountability is to the group, more than to externally imposed accountability measures; group accountability and self-accountability are powerful influences on the learning community's ethos and action.

Leadership and outside influence

14 Leadership outside and inside the group is important in stimulating and facilitating the learning community.
15 While learning communities can develop without stimulus or action from above or outside, assistance, guidance, resources and encouragement from others within and in some cases outside the organisation can facilitate the learning process.

Overall dynamics

16 Time, place, space and language are important elements in creating a learning community.
17 Overall, what seems to work most effectively is a combination of external understanding, advice, assistance and recognition ('top-down'), coupled with a focus on internal issues and solutions, with teacher and group learning to address these through empowerment and with internal action and accountability ('bottom-up').

Implications and conclusions

The research evidence on learning communities and how these can support teachers' professional learning and improve student achievement is encouraging.

Not surprisingly, there are many who advocate the development of learning communities as means of lifting educational performance. In this age, we have grown accustomed to demanding quick fixes and solutions to problems, what could be termed the '24-hour help desk mentality'. However, learning communities cannot be mandated, imposed, built or operated in a technical, mechanistic sense. Rather, these need to be encouraged, nourished and sustained in the manner of an organic system, hence the interest in ecological approaches.

Building a learning community is more like agriculture or gardening than engineering or chemistry. While agriculture is underpinned by both engineering and chemistry, it is a far more inexact and varied undertaking, heavily dependent on the local and wider environment and reliant on knowledge, learning and judgement.

Some organisations and groups appear to suffer from learning disabilities.[19] These disabilities need to be diagnosed, assessed and addressed through suitable interventions in the same ways in which we would help a student.

As noted, educational leaders cannot, nor should they attempt to mandate or force the development of learning communities. As Andy Hargreaves has noted, collegiality should not be contrived or forced.[20] Leaders can, however, assist organisational members to come together, focus and collaborate on issues of importance. Educational leaders need to ensure that teaching and learning are central concerns of the educational organisation and do all in their power to ensure that nothing is allowed to obstruct or distort this central focus.

There is a challenge for educational leaders to deal with situations where learning has atrophied. As McBeath has noted:

> It is hard for teachers to shed an outer skin which has calcified over many years in the classroom where dialogue is a rare commodity no matter how hard teachers strive for it, and in which 'instruction' is the norm.[21]

Educational leaders within and outside the group need to act judiciously to wear away this 'outer skin' so that learning can once again flourish. However, building a learning community should not be construed as being about 'fixing' teachers. Educational leaders should look to themselves, their strengths, weaknesses and actions, as well as to others, for problems and solutions.

The voluntary and empowering nature of learning communities is important. In our evaluation of the AGQTP, while we were very positive about the outcomes of the projects and the overall program, our strong recommendation to the Department of Education and Training in NSW was that the program should retain its voluntary status. To make it compulsory would almost guarantee failure or 'lip-service' in many schools while being very costly if the current model of teacher-release was continued.

One of the most encouraging outcomes of these and other related studies has been the extent to which dialogue about and focus on quality teaching have emerged and been seen to reinvigorate jaded, mid-to-late career teachers who are now active participants in learning communities. Other teachers, of course, have never stopped learning.

Another important outcome of the case studies is the degree to which latent leadership potential has been released through the development of the learning communities, in turn providing both a stimulus and resource for further change and improvement.

Finally, to complete the circle, what the various studies and work by others have confirmed is that teachers and groups of teachers can learn, and are more 'made' than 'born', although the 'making' needs to continue career-long. It seems that it is never too late to nourish the learning community if the right conditions are provided.

What follows in an appendix is a brief elaboration on action learning. Chapter 7 then considers the issue of leading change in schools.

Acknowledgements

In addition to the acknowledgements made previously regarding the NSW HSC successful teaching study and the AESOP study, the contribution of Peter Aubusson and Laurie Brady, my co-researchers and writers on the AGQTP evaluation, is acknowledged. I would also like to acknowledge Norman McCulla and Catherine Scott, co-researchers and writers on the NSW QTA research study, and other members of the QTA steering committee for their contributions.

Action learning

The AGQTP evaluation described in this chapter was concerned with action learning, rather than its near relative, action research.

Action learning can be defined as a process through which people come together to learn from each other and share their experience.[22] While this has always happened informally in organisations, we now tend to think of action learning as involving a team of people addressing a common task or problem. There may or may not be an external coach, critical friend, mentor, or facilitator, although this is increasingly the case.

Action research tends to be a more formal, structured approach to problem solving involving practitioners. Action learning has tended to be used more in the corporate sphere,[23] while action research has been more commonly used in education and community settings. Increasingly, however, the two terms have blurred and are used interchangeably across a variety of settings. A related methodology is that of experiential learning which, as above, can be ad hoc or more formal, and with some form of external facilitation or input.

In action learning, action research, and experiential learning, a key aspect is that of a cycle of reflection and action. If improvement is desired, then the cycle tends to repeat, namely, reflection-action-review-reflection-action, and so forth.[24] Each step informs subsequent steps, and ideally an upward cycle of improvement is set in motion.

Action learning provides an appropriate and sustainable way of building the capacity of schools to improve practice. It is improvement-oriented, interactive, uses multiple methods and is characterised by validity, viewed as constructing, testing, sharing, and retesting exemplars of teaching.[25]

Some of the advantages of action learning are those of inclusiveness, flexibility, respect for the knowledge and experience of participants, involvement, collegiality, empowerment, and ownership. Challenges include building the capacity of schools to support action learning, maintaining commitment, developing effective leadership, creating productive partnership with mentors (where involved), and extending participation from small teams of key personnel to a whole school engagement with professional learning.

Notes

1 Toole, J. C., & Louis, K. S. The role of professional learning communities in international education. In Leithwood, K., & Hallinger, P. (Eds.). (2002). *Second international handbook of educational leadership and administration* (pp. 245–279). Dordrecht: Kluwer.
2 Darling-Hammond, L. (2006). *Powerful teacher education* (p. ix). San Francisco: Jossey-Bass.
3 Scott, C., & Dinham, S. (2008). Born not made: The nativist myth and teachers thinking. *Teacher Development, 12*(2), 115–124.
4 Reynolds, D., Teddlie, C., Creemers, B., Scheerens, J., & Townsend, T. An introduction to school effectiveness research, In Teddlie, C., & Reynolds, D. (Eds.). (2000). *The international handbook of school effectiveness research* (pp. 3–25). London: Falmer.
5 Busher, H., & Harris, A. (2000). *Subject leadership and school improvement*. London: Paul Chapman; Gronn, P. Distributed Leadership. In Leithwood, K., & Hallinger, P. (Eds.). (2002). *Second international handbook of educational leadership and administration* (pp. 653–696). Dordrecht: Kluwer; Spillane, J., Halverson, R., & Diamond, J. (2001). Investigating school leadership practice: A distributed perspective. *Educational Researcher, 30*(3), 23–28; York-Barr, J., & Duke, K. (2004). What do we know about teacher leadership? Findings from two decades of scholarship. *Review of Educational Research, 74*(3), 255–316;

Dinham, S. (2007). The secondary head of department and the achievement of exceptional student outcomes. *Journal of Educational Administration, 45*(1), 62–79; see also (2008). *Journal of Educational Administration, 46*(2), thematic edition on distributed leadership.
6 Hattie, J. (2003). *Teachers make a difference: What is the research difference?* Available at: http://www.acer.edu.au/workshops/documents/Teachers_Make_a_Difference_Hattie.pdf
7 Senge, P. M. (1990). *The fifth discipline.* Sydney: Random House, Australia.
8 Kilpatrick, S., Barrett, M., & Jones, T. (2003). Defining learning communities. Paper presented to NZARE/AARE international conference, Auckland, 30 November – 3 December.
9 Watson, K., & Steele, F. (2006). Building a teacher education community: Recognising the ecological reality of sustainable collaboration. *Asia-Pacific Forum on Science Learning and Teaching, 7*(1), n.p. Available at http://www.ied.edu.hk/apfslt/v7_issue1/watson/watson2.htm
10 Voulalas, Z. D., & Sharpe, F. (2005). Creating schools as learning communities: Obstacles and processes. *Journal of Educational Administration, 43*(2), 187–208.
11 Ayres, P., Dinham, S., & Sawyer, W. (1999). *Successful teaching in the NSW Higher School Certificate.* Sydney: NSW Department of Education and Training; Ayres, P., Dinham, S., & Sawyer, W. (1998). *The identification of successful teaching methodologies in the NSW Higher School Certificate: A research report for the NSW Department of Education and Training.* Penrith: University of Western Sydney, Nepean; Ayres, P., Dinham, S., & Sawyer, W. (2000). Successful senior secondary teaching, *Quality Teaching Series, No. 1*, Australian College of Education, September 1–20; Ayres, P., Dinham, S., & Sawyer, W. (2004). Effective teaching in the context of a Grade 12 high stakes external examination in New South Wales, Australia. *British Educational Research Journal, 30*(1), 141–165; Ayres, P., Dinham, S., & Sawyer, W. (1997). *The identification of successful teaching methodologies in the NSW higher school certificate: Identifying the successful teachers.* Penrith: University of Western Sydney, Nepean; Sawyer, W., Ayres, P., & Dinham, S. (2001). What does an effective Year 12 English teacher look like? *English in Australia, 129*(30), 51–63.
12 NSW Department of Education and Training. (2003). *Quality teaching in NSW public schools: Discussion paper.* Sydney: Professional Support and Curriculum Directorate, NSW DET.
13 See Aubusson, P., Brady, L., & Dinham, S. (2005). *Action learning: What works? A research report prepared for the New South Wales Department of Education and Training.* Sydney: University of Technology Sydney; Brady, L., Aubusson, P., & Dinham, S. (2006). Action learning for school improvement. *Educational Practice and Theory, 28*(2), 27–39; Dinham, S., Aubusson, P., & Brady, L. (2008). Distributed leadership as a factor in and outcome of teacher action learning. *International Electronic Journal for Leadership in Learning, 12*(4). Available at: http://www.ucalgary.ca/~iejll/volume12/dinham.htm; Aubusson, P., Steele, F., Dinham, S., & Brady, L. (2007). Action learning in teacher learning community formation: Informative or transformative? *Teacher Development, 11*(2), 133–148; Brady, L., Aubusson, P., & Dinham, S. (2008). Action learning: Contemporary professional development, *Curriculum and Teaching, 23*(1), 5–19; Aubusson, P.,

Dinham, S., Ewing, R., & Ewing, R. *Action learning for sustainable professional development*. London: Routledge (in press).

14 Dinham, S., Aubusson, P., & Brady, L. (2008). Distributed leadership as a factor in and outcome of teacher action learning, *International Electronic Journal for Leadership in Learning*, 12(4). Available at: http://www.ucalgary.ca/~iejll/volume12/dinham.htm

15 Dinham, S. (2002). NSW Quality Teaching Awards – Research, rigour and transparency. *Unicorn*, 28(1), 5–9.

16 Brock, P. (2000). *Standards of professional practice for accomplished teaching in Australian classrooms*. Canberra: Australian College of Educators/Australian Association for Research in Education/Australian Curriculum Studies Association.

17 Bergin, M., Dinham, S., Scott, C., & Brock, P. (2002). *The heart of teaching: Report on the 2001 quality teaching awards project*. Sydney: Australian College of Educators, NSW Chapter; Dinham, S. (2002). NSW Quality Teaching Awards – Research, rigour and transparency, *Unicorn*, 28(1), 5–9; Dinham, S., & Scott, C. (2003). Benefits to teachers of the professional learning portfolio: A case study. *Teacher Development*, 7(3), 187–202; Dinham, S., & Scott, C. (2003). Awards for teaching excellence: Intentions and realities. *Unicorn Online Refereed Article*, No. 24, 1–25; Scott, C., McCulla, N., & Dinham, S. (2007). The ecology of quality teaching. Paper presented to the British Educational Research Association Annual Conference, Institute of Education, University of London, September; McCulla, N., Dinham, S., & Scott, C. (2007). Stepping out from the crowd: Some findings from the NSW quality teaching awards on seeking recognition for professional accomplishment.*Unicorn Online Refereed Article*, ORA 51, 3–32.

18 MacBeath, J. (2006). Leadership as a subversive activity. *ACEL Monograph Series*, Number 39.

19 Senge, P. M. (1990). *The fifth discipline*. Sydney: Random House, Australia; Bhindi, N. (2007). Why workplaces resist learning. Paper presented to the Sixth International Conference on Educational Leadership, Australian Centre for Educational Leadership, University of Wollongong, 15–16 February.

20 Hargreaves, A. (1994). *Changing teachers, changing times*. London: Cassell.

21 MacBeath, J. (2006). Leadership as a subversive activity. *ACEL Monograph Series*, No. 39, p. 19.

22 Dick, B. (1997). *Action learning and action research*. Retrieved September 2, 2005, from www.scu.edu.au/schools/gcm/ar/arp/actlearn.html

23 See Mumford, A. (1995). Learning in action. *Industrial and commercial training*, 27(8), 36–40; Koo, L. C. (1999). Learning action learning, *Journal of Workplace Learning*, 11(3), 89–94.

24 See Dick, B. (1997). *Action learning and action research*. Retrieved September 2, 2005, from www.scu.edu.au/schools/gcm/ar/arp/actlearn.html

25 LaBoskey V. K. (2004). The methodology of self-study and its theoretical underpinnings. In Loughran, J. J., Hamilton, M. L., LaBoskey, V. K., & Russell, T. (Eds.). *International Handbook of Self-study of Teaching and Teacher Education Practices* (pp. 814–817). Dordrecht: Kluwer.

7 | Making change happen and keeping it going

Mere change is not growth. Growth is the synthesis of change and continuity, and where there is no continuity there is no growth.

(C.S. Lewis)

Introduction

The purpose of this chapter is to give you some additional guidance to assist with the process of educational change. The previous chapters were based largely on research projects with which I've been involved. This chapter draws on additional material on change, both from education and the broader sphere of organisational change.

Once again, I have provided references should you wish to consult the original sources in more detail.

The nature of change

Some simple definitions[1]

- *Change:* a difference or departure from the status quo
- *Change process:* the process by which an individual, group, or organisation attempts to achieve change
- *Effects of change:* the impact or consequences of achieved change.

Forces for change

Many of the forces for change experienced by schools and other organisations are largely external.[2] Some of these key forces are:

- economic
- social

- political
- ideological
- technological, and (increasingly)
- environmental.

People and organisations can react in a variety of ways to such change pressures, depending upon the nature of the individual change and their general predisposition towards change. For example, some people will:

- see change as a threat to their power base, responsibilities and autonomy
- feel uneasy about the risk and possible failure associated with the change
- be deterred by the pressure to do 'more with less' or even with the same resources
- feel undervalued or devalued by what is being proposed
- find potential disruptions to established procedures and even traditions threatening.

The culture and climate of the organisation and the experience and views of individuals and groups within it towards change will be important in determining reactions and responses to change, responses which can be both emotional and behavioural.

One thing that decades of pressure for change and rising external criticisms have done to some schools and individuals is to create a climate of mistrust and avoidance of change. I have interviewed and spoken with several principals who had taken over risk- and change-averse schools. Previous principals, possibly because they knew they would be retiring soon, had kept change at bay as much as possible, so that when these new principals took over they were faced with a situation where some fairly substantial and unsettling changes had to be instituted immediately if the school was to fulfil its responsibilities and meet various accountabilities. This situation got these principals 'offside' with their new staff as the 'roadblocks' to change were hurriedly removed and their 'new broom' raised a cloud of dust.

It was seen in the AESOP study sites, however, how successful faculties, teams and schools had positive attitudes towards change, and that rather than perceiving change as a threat, they looked for the benefits available to them from being associated with new programs and initiatives. As noted, change is often about changing people – what they know, what they can do and their outlook and approach.

A consistent theme in this book is that leadership and professional learning play important roles in changing people and in changing matters such as policies, structures, processes, programs and ultimately, in re-culturing schools.

Groupthink and Balkanisation

Group dynamics play an important role in how individuals and organisations respond to change. One concept that I have found useful in understanding group behaviour and reactions to change is that of 'groupthink'. The term was first coined by William Whyte in the early 1950s and refined and popularised by Irving Janis in the early 1970s in his book *Victims of groupthink* and in other work.[3]

Groupthink involves 'in-groups' and 'out-groups', and those who are in the in-group exhibit a high degree of unanimity, with the group's decision making and behaviour being dysfunctional or sub-optimal in its interrelationship with the rest of the organisation. The group tends to police its members in various ways and to filter out or distort information coming into the group. As a result, while the group may appear on some levels to be operating rationally in terms of its norms and internal rules for operation, its decision making and performance are faulty, as the group does not consider all information and alternative courses of action rationally and objectively.

It should be noted that groupthink can occur within existing formal groups where all or some of the formal group exhibit groupthink symptoms. Alternatively, the members can be drawn from different formal groups across the organisation because of what members have in common. Levels of an organisation such as an executive made up of senior staff can also exhibit and be inflicted by groupthink. It is possible for whole organisations, even governments, to be under the influence of groupthink. For example, some would classify the 'Cold War' as groupthink on a global scale.

Janis noted that members' cohesion is an important precondition of groupthink, although not all cohesive groups are dysfunctional. History also plays a part in the development of groupthink and some of the examples of groupthink I have encountered in my career in education had histories to rival the Middle East or Northern Ireland. No one could remember how the group came into existence, or why it was so opposed to others in the organisation, but there was clearly a defined group membership and identity recognised by those inside and outside the group.

There are a variety of possible causes of groupthink, some of which may operate conjointly:

- There was possibly a lack of 'objective' or 'authoritative' leadership in the past.
- The group may have formed in response to external threats or conflict.
- Perhaps members of the group shared similar social backgrounds or interests.

- Members of the group may have been geographically isolated from the rest of the organisation.
- Perhaps there was an ideological split in the organisation.
- Members of the group were kept isolated or bypassed by those in charge.

Whatever the causes, small initial differences can become larger under groupthink, so that divisions between groups can become wider, deeper, more clearly defined and harder to bridge over time.

To help you identify groupthink, Whyte, Janis and other researchers have noted the following 'symptoms' or groupthink behaviours:

- filtering and distorting information coming into the group
- self-belief in the group's righteousness and 'morality'
- exerting pressure on those within the group to conform and not speak out
- use of 'mindguards' to protect the group from outside information that might threaten or harm the group
- failure to consider all alternatives and consequences objectively and rationally
- rationalising group dysfunctionality and poor decision making
- seeing and portraying other individuals and groups in stereotypical ways; deriding and attacking the views and positions of others
- members suppressing true feelings; don't question ideas of other members openly; may be in awe or fear of influential group leaders
- group seeing itself in a struggle for survival; may see itself as invulnerable
- 'escalation of commitment', in that the group continues to pursue an increasingly destructive, harmful path or conflict, and even increases its commitment, despite evidence that it is failing; adopting a 'crash or crash through' approach[4]
- projecting an image of unity to outside world; votes as a 'bloc' in meetings and decision making and 'hunts as a pack'.

Dealing with groupthink

Most researchers and writers advocate some form of outside intervention to break open the solidarity of the group and to let light and air into the situation when dealing with groupthink. For example:

- Form some type of matrix structure within the organisation so that group members become members of other groups to work on issues, tasks or problems and in doing so, widen their understanding of the organisation.
- Where there is a formal group such as a faculty experiencing groupthink, appoint an external evaluator or facilitator to speak with all members confidentially, conduct 'reality testing' and report back to the group.
- Confront the ideas of the group rationally, keeping personalities and histories out of the discussion; emphasise use of fact and evidence.

- Meet with group members individually; seek their input, ideas, reactions and test these with the group membership without 'naming names'.
- Commend members of the group publicly for their achievements, even (and especially) if the group culture and norms reject recognition of its members.
- Refuse to take sides or listen to accounts of past 'disasters' or 'wars'; be scrupulously fair in dealing with the group and its members.
- Use external experts to provide information, alternatives, assistance.
- Break up some of the social 'glue' of the group; selectively invite members to social occasions with other staff; invite members to join with other staff on projects as above.
- If all else fails: issue an ultimatum; break up the group operationally/ geographically; appoint a new leader; restructure; transfer some staff.

Groupthink is a continuum with elements present in all organisations. It is useful if you are attuned to the history of the organisation and sensitive to the symptoms of groupthink. Forming productive, professional relationships with all group members may be difficult, especially the case-hardened 'blockers' (see later), but you need to make the effort.

Balkanisation

Balkanisation can be defined as the breakdown or fragmentation of a region, division or organisation into smaller formal and informal units. It owes its name to the political fragmentation and reformation of the Balkan states that occurred over several centuries.

Various researchers and commentators have written on the fact that fragmentation is a phenomenon found in many schools, especially secondary schools with their traditional divisions or 'silos' based on subject specialisation. Andy Hargreaves applied the term 'Balkanisation' in his book *Changing teachers, changing times* in 1994. He noted that in schools there were identifiable patterns of teachers' relationships and that:

> In balkanised cultures, these patterns mainly consist of teachers working neither in isolation, nor with most of their colleagues as a whole school, but in smaller sub-groups within the school community, such as secondary school subject departments, special needs units, or junior and senior primary divisions within the elementary school.[5]

As with cohesion – a feature or precondition of groupthink, but desirable outside that context – there is nothing inherently wrong with teachers working together in small groups. In fact, it is desirable. The problem arises when teachers working in these small groups are isolated and insulated from those in other groups and it is in this situation where groupthink can develop and take hold, with members' main loyalties and efforts directed towards the group, rather than to the organisation as a whole and its clients.

Overcoming resistance to change

The organisational and educational change literatures emphasise that participation, information, education, communication, involvement, support and agreement are all necessary means for overcoming resistance to change.

McLagen offers five strategies for success with change:

1. Be sure the change will add value.
2. Match the change process with the change.
3. Provide management support.
4. Prepare the system for change.
5. Help people align (to the change agenda).[6]

As mentioned, it is commonly agreed that people are the key to successful change. Smith has noted:

> *It is people who make up organisations and it is they who are the real source of, and vehicle for, change. They are the ones who will either embrace or resist change. If organisational change is to take hold and succeed then organisations and the people who work in them must be readied for such transformation. Change readiness is not automatic and it cannot be assumed. A failure to assess organisational and individual change readiness may result in managers spending significant time and energy dealing with resistance to change. By creating change readiness before attempts at organisational renewal begin the need for later action to cope with resistance may be largely avoided. An investment in developing change readiness – at both an individual and whole-of-organisation level – can achieve a double benefit. Positive energy goes into creating preparedness for the changes and, in turn, there can be a significant reduction in the need for management of resistance once organisational revival is underway.*[7]

Smith has identified three key steps in creating readiness for change:

- creating a sense of need and urgency for change
- communicating the change message and ensuring participation and involvement in the change process
- providing anchoring points and a base for the achievement of change.[8]

Pennington suggests that proposed changes can be placed along two scales: radical–incremental and core–peripheral (see Figure 7.1). Plotting the character of a proposed change along these scales can provide a sense of how difficult the introduction of any particular initiative might be and how much 'disturbance' to the status quo it might require and generate.

- *Radical changes* to an institution's or department's core business will normally generate higher levels of disturbance and be associated with higher levels of risk
- *Incremental changes* to peripheral activities are often considered to be unexceptional ('fine tuning') with low disturbance and low risk and can be accommodated as a matter of course, especially if the group involved has a successful past record of continuous improvement.

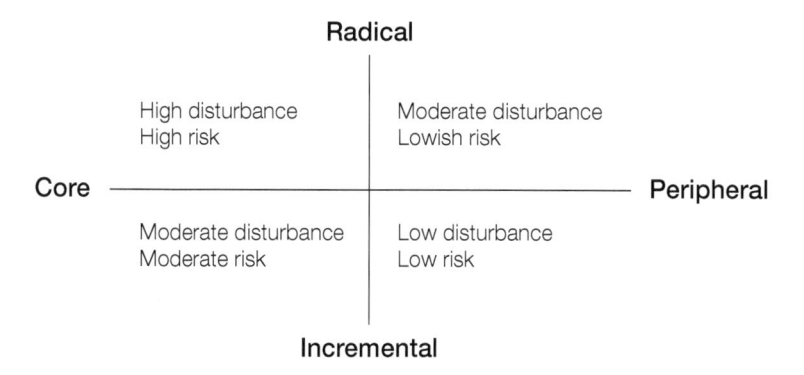

```
                        Radical
                          |
      High disturbance    |   Moderate disturbance
      High risk           |   Lowish risk
                          |
Core ─────────────────────┼───────────────────── Peripheral
                          |
      Moderate disturbance|   Low disturbance
      Moderate risk       |   Low risk
                          |
                      Incremental
```

Figure 7.1 Radical and incremental change (Pennington)

Pennington notes that, as a general rule, professionals and technical staff will tend to resist changes which are perceived to threaten their core values and practices, those which have a negative impact on individuals, and those which diminish group autonomy.[9]

Counting the numbers in educational change[10]

In politics, having 'the numbers' or the support of the membership for any initiative is essential. In educational change, the numbers are equally important.

In considering the likely success of any desired change, it is useful for educational leaders to consider the membership of three broad groups:

1 *Enthusiasts:* supporters for the change who will be prepared to commit time and effort to the initiative. Enthusiasts range from the informed and 'hard-headed' to the naïve. Enthusiasts may have experience and expertise in the area or may be prepared to 'give it a go' if such familiarity is lacking. Enthusiasts tend to be early adopters and risk takers, although sometimes they let their heart rule their head. There

are two sub-groups of enthusiasts: those who will cheerfully support almost anything, and those who will provide support for a particular issue. Enthusiasts can also be initiators of change.

2 *Watchers:* as the name implies, these people are more calculative and are open to persuasion. They are generally compliant. Watchers are prepared to consider a change on its merits. As with enthusiasts, they will go along with a leader who has won their respect and trust, suspending judgement until later. Watchers can go either way on an issue. Over time, they can become increasingly involved and supportive if they are exposed to convincing evidence and argument. Small successes can bring watchers onside. However, if the change process is handled badly, watchers can withdraw their support and involvement and may even join the third group.

3 *Blockers:* blockers may be opposed to a particular change, or change in general. They can be active or passive in their opposition. They will not be swayed by rational argument or evidence and can be counted on to resist change. Even if their opposition is muted, members of this group may use their influence with others to obstruct and 'white ant' or sabotage the change. Alternatively, they may say little but will studiously ignore the change, waiting for it, and you, to go away. Blockers may have been in the school or system for some time, their views having hardened over the years. 'Balkanisation' and 'groupthink' can govern the thinking and actions of blockers. Blockers tend to police each other and filter out and distort unwelcome information. In some cases, there may be different groups of blockers who actually oppose each other.

Both the composition of the above groups and the number of people each contains can be significant in the success of educational change. For example, if the blockers comprise a small number of highly influential people, the desired change could be doomed before it starts or undermined once it begins.

In an overall group of 20, five enthusiasts and 10 watchers could be enough of a critical mass to see a change through. However, eight enthusiasts and eight blockers would indicate polarisation of staff, with conflict and failure likely.

As an educational leader, it is instructive to reflect on the numbers of each group for any proposed change. Knowledge of the organisation's history, culture and group dynamics are also important. Past failed attempts at change need to be understood and considered as some blockers act as 'keepers of the nightmare' (see Deal and Patterson later) – 'we tried that in 1975 and it didn't work', and so forth. Of course, blockers ignore their own roles in such failures.

Schools and other educational institutions are not democracies, however, and leaders have to make unpopular decisions at times for the overall good of the organisation. Additionally, much change is mandated and the real issue is how to accommodate change of this nature and use it to the organisation's advantage. When it comes to decision making, the most effective educational leaders possess each of these capacities, being both courageous and strategic, as we have seen in discussion of the AESOP study findings.[11]

The evaluation of the Australian Government Quality Teaching Program (AGQTP) mentioned previously highlighted the importance of leaders carefully considering the composition and influence of groups.[12] In forming AGQTP action learning teams, principals thoughtfully and strategically selected project team leaders and encouraged and 'massaged' team membership. In several cases, principals admitted to having induced key watchers and potential blockers to join project teams, operating on the Lyndon B. Johnson theory that it would be better to have these people 'inside the tent' than out. These principals reasoned that once such people had become involved and had developed a personal stake in the projects, they would influence others to provide support or at least to give the projects 'a fair go'; that is, their commitment would escalate, this time with positive consequences.

In the AESOP study, some successful principals had made the decision to bypass the blockers altogether. They concentrated on encouraging, professionally developing and empowering groups of enthusiasts and watchers, hoping to achieve contagion effects from successful change across the wider school. There is a danger in this, in that the leader can be accused of 'playing favourites', but the bigger danger is that nothing happens.[13]

A key aspect in all of this is knowing one's fellow staff – and, where relevant, community – members and how each might react to any change in the status quo. Over time, successfully managed change (and retirements and transfers) can see the weakening of the blockers' power base and the overcoming of a culture of negativity and resistance.[14]

A final point for educational leaders to consider: don't take the opposition of the blockers too personally. Their behaviour is frequently irrational and the result of personal, group and organisational history. Their opposition is almost a vote of confidence in, and a character reference for you.

Why does change go wrong?

One of the fundamental errors in perception is that change is about management and managing change. The term 'change management' is misleading. The various studies cited in this book, including the AESOP study and the AGQTP evaluation, showed that successful change is much more about *active leadership of people* than *management of systems*.

Particularly where change is in the high-disturbance/high-risk and moderate-disturbance/moderate-risk quadrants identified by Pennington, a number of things are likely to happen which can compromise the change effort and progress. Each was evident to some degree in the AGQTP evaluation described previously:

- Getting started is difficult.
- Maintaining momentum takes effort.
- Progress is slower than expected.
- Goals and targets need revision (usually downwards).
- Direction changes.
- Setbacks occur.
- Evidence to judge progress and improved performance is lacking.
- Criticism and doubt emerge.

To help us understand why these problems occur, Kotter, who studied the change experiences of over 100 companies, noted a number of common errors:

1. not establishing a great enough sense of urgency
2. not creating a powerful enough guiding coalition
3. lacking a vision
4. under-communicating the vision by a factor of ten
5. not removing obstacles to the new vision
6. not systematically planning for and creating short-term wins
7. declaring victory too soon
8. not anchoring changes in the corporation's culture.

Kotter found:

> In the final analysis, change sticks when it becomes 'the way we do things around here', when it seeps into the bloodstream of the corporate body. Until new behaviours are rooted in social norms and shared values, they are subject to degradation as soon as the pressure for change is removed.
>
> Two factors are particularly important in institutionalising change in corporate culture. The first is a conscious attempt to show people how the new approaches, behaviours, and attitudes have helped improve performance. When people are left on their own to make the connections, they sometimes create very inaccurate links ...
>
> The second factor is taking sufficient time to make sure that the next generation of top management really does personify the new approach ... One bad succession decision at the top of an organization can undermine a decade of hard work.[15]

The above observations on where change goes wrong and what is needed to make it 'stick' ring true in the light of the research with which I've been involved. The key aspects appear to centre on:

- getting people engaged and empowered to tackle the change
- communicating and selling the change
- providing the necessary professional learning and development
- leading, encouraging and defending the change
- using evidence to monitor, evaluate and modify the change effort
- celebrating and communicating successes.

Importance of school culture

You can't hope to work in or change schools without coming up against school culture.

I have visited many schools over the years. As experienced educators, when we go into a school we quickly make a series of judgements based on a range of evidence, observations and cues. The problem for people who have spent a long time in a school is that these cues are no longer seen – they develop organisational myopia, unseeingly stepping over the 'dead dogs' in the corridor and failing to recognise the 'elephant in the room' or the 'wood from the trees'.

The implication here is that we need to stand back periodically and view our organisation from the eyes of a stranger or visitor. What we see, hear and feel will be important indicators of the culture and health of our organisation. I suggest to my postgraduate students who are school leaders that they visit each other's schools and give feedback on what they see as an outsider. I also suggest that they telephone their own school – disguising their voice, and ask for help. The reception they receive will be instructive.

Organisational climate and culture

There are a variety of definitions of organisational climate and culture. Climate is basically the day-to-day 'feel' of the organisation and our judgement of climate is based largely on observable features, events and behaviours. Climate can change fairly readily, for good or bad, under the influence of leadership.

Culture, on the other hand, is deeper, harder to read and harder to change. It is usually considered to comprise the behavioural norms, assumptions and beliefs of an organisation developed over longer periods of time, sometimes generations, and even centuries in the case of some long-established schools and other organisations.

These norms, values and beliefs may be unspoken, largely unquestioned and constantly reinforced for people both consciously and unconsciously.

McBrien and Brandt have offered the following definitions and explanations:

> *School culture and climate refers to the sum of the values, cultures, safety practices, and organizational structures within a school that cause it to function and react in particular ways. Some schools are said to have a nurturing environment that recognizes children and treats them as individuals; others may have the feel of authoritarian structures where rules are strictly enforced and hierarchical control is strong. Teaching practices, diversity, and the relationships among administrators, teachers, parents, and students contribute to school climate. Although the two terms are somewhat interchangeable, school climate refers mostly to the school's effects on students, while school culture refers more to the way teachers and other staff members work together.*[16]

The work of Schein has been important in our understanding of organisational culture, which he has defined as:

> *A pattern of shared basic assumptions that the group learned as it solved its problems of external adaptation and internal integration, that has worked well enough to be considered valid and, therefore, to be taught to new members as the correct way to perceive, think, and feel in relation to those problems.*[17]

Schein discerned three levels of organisational culture, resembling an iceberg:

- *Level 1: Tangible elements* (artifacts and creations); includes verbal, visual, behavioural manifestations *(the tip of the iceberg).*
- *Level 2: Values and beliefs;* mission statements, philosophy, credo *(above the water line and partly visible below the surface).*
- *Level 3: Underlying assumptions;* taken for granted assumptions; invisible, deep-seated, subconscious assumptions about human nature, relationships, reality *(under the water and out of sight).*

As a new leader, it takes time to tune in to, dig down and understand the culture of a school, particularly coming to an understanding of Level 3 above, which those who have been at the school longer than you may be unable to articulate beyond the simple observation that 'it's the way we do things around here'.[18] New arrivals may not be taught about the culture in any overt way but rather, slowly tune into it. On the other hand, what they or you might be told may not fit with contemporary reality.

Regardless, people tend to absorb the culture as they interact with others and take part in day-to-day school life.

Where schools have control over hiring of staff, there may be a conscious effort to select and screen applicants for positions based upon their perceived 'fit' with the school's culture. Those employed who don't fit the culture and who can't or won't change their views, may feel that they don't belong, which could lead to conflict or resignation.

In their book *Transforming schools*, Zmuda, Kuklis and Kline offer six steps of continuous improvement in schools which begin with recognition of school culture:

1. Identify and clarify the core beliefs that define the school's culture.
2. Create a shared vision by explicitly defining what these core beliefs will look like in practice.
3. Collect accurate, detailed data and use analysis of the data to define where the school is now and to determine the gaps between the current reality and the shared vision.
4. Identify the innovation(s) that will most likely close the gaps between the current reality and the shared vision.
5. Develop and implement an action plan that supports teachers through the change process and integrates the innovation within each classroom and throughout the school.
6. Embrace collective autonomy as the only way to close the gaps and embrace collective accountability in establishing responsibility for closing the gaps.[19]

Similarly, Deal and Patterson in their book *Shaping school culture*[20] have identified eight major symbolic roles for leaders seeking to build strong and cohesive school cultures:

1. *Historian:* seeks to understand the social and normative past of the school.
2. *Anthropological sleuth:* analyses and probes for the current set of norms, values and beliefs that define the current culture.
3. *Visionary:* works with other leaders and the community to define a deeply value-focused picture of the future for the school; has a constantly evolving vision.
4. *Symbol:* affirms values through dress, behaviour, attention, routines.
5. *Potter:* shapes and is shaped by the school's heroes, rituals, traditions, ceremonies, symbols; brings in members of staff who share core values.
6. *Poet:* uses language to reinforce values and sustains the school's best image of itself.

7 *Actor:* improvises in the school's inevitable dramas, comedies and tragedies.
8 *Healer:* oversees transitions and change in the life of the school; heals the wounds of conflict and loss.

Deal and Patterson conceptualise schools as tribes and note that many school leaders inherit a dysfunctional, divided, inter-tribal mess. They come up against and must engage with 'toxic' school cultures and sub-cultures.

Characteristics of toxic school cultures include staff and the school as a whole being focused on negative values (making the school better for staff; serving only an elite group of students; focusing on unimportant/less important outcomes). Meaning for members of the 'tribe' is derived from sub-culture membership, anti-student, anti-system and anti-community sentiments, or life outside work (golf, gardening, sport, food and wine – anything except teaching). People soaked in toxic school cultures may behave quite differently out of school, being seemingly different people.

In toxic schools:

- The elements of culture reinforce negativity.
- Values and beliefs are negative.
- The culture works against anything that is positive.
- Rituals and traditions are phony, joyless, counterproductive.

Powerful sub-culture members become:

- Negaholics
- Saboteurs
- Pessimistic story tellers
- 'Keepers of the nightmare'
- Prima donnas
- Space cadets
- Martyrs
- Driftwood, dead wood and ballast.

Deal and Patterson's 'antidotes for negativism' include:

- Confront the negativity head on – give people a chance to vent their venom in a public forum (listen, challenge, then wait for more positive elements to emerge).
- Shield and support positive cultural elements and staff.
- Focus attention on the recruitment, selection and retention of effective, positive staff – replace chronic negaholics.
- Rabidly celebrate the positive and the possible.
- Consciously and directly focus on eradicating the negative and rebuilding around positive norms and beliefs.

- Develop new stories of success, renewal and accomplishment.
- Help those who might succeed and thrive in a new school to make the move.

As a leader, coming to an appreciation of your school's culture is vital. You need to understand where it's been, and where it's at, if you are to take your school to where you want it to go. Likewise, you need to understand where people are coming from if you hope to lead them somewhere else.

The successful leaders profiled previously attended to all three of Schein's levels, ranging from their attention to school vision, down to management of daily events and everything in between. They were also able to recognise the symptoms and causes of negativism identified by Deal and Patterson, seeking to drive out negative attitudes and behaviours and modelling a positive approach and mindset. They were relentless in 'talking up' the school, its students and staff.

Managing conflict and change

It would be misleading and unrealistic to suggest that change doesn't involve conflict. Any time people are put together, there is the potential for conflict.

Conflict is usually defined as some form of incompatibility of views between individuals or groups who then engage in a process to accommodate these differences. (There can also be internal conflict over the course of action on an issue, where an individual is faced with choice.) Where one side attempts to see its view or position triumph, this can result in a 'win–lose' situation (see below), which can sow the seeds for later and continuing conflict, with Balkanisation and groupthink possible outcomes.

It should also be stated that some people seem to thrive on drama and conflict. Some people I've worked with were capable of starting a fight in an empty room.

The bureaucratic view of conflict as espoused by Max Weber – the German political economist and sociologist who published numerous influential papers in the late 19th and early 20th centuries – was that organisational conflict could be overcome, or better still avoided, by rules and procedures – bureaucratic systems – that impersonally and objectively governed the behaviour of all employees.

However, other writers such as Mary Parker Follett – an American social worker, consultant and writer whose career overlapped with that of Weber and who introduced the term 'conflict resolution' – have seen conflict as a necessary accompaniment to change and the development of new ideas and approaches.[21] Under this view, leaders should not strive to eliminate or keep a lid on conflict, but to use it productively to question accepted practices and find innovative solutions.

'Win–win', 'win–lose', and 'lose–lose' strategies

The origins of 'win–win' and 'win–lose' – and 'lose–lose' – strategies lie in game theory. Today, they are also associated with situations where different approaches to conflict resolution can result in differing outcomes.

With a 'win–win' approach, each side emerges with 'face' intact, largely because the conflict has been depersonalised, with each party demonstrating flexibility, honesty and communicating openly in seeking creative solutions to the conflict. The good of the organisation and its clients are usually the most important considerations in this situation.

With a 'win–lose' situation, however, each side defines and sees the matter in those terms and pursues its own goals, rather than higher organisational goals. It becomes a contest of wills and force, with each side seeking to damage the other's case and emerge victorious. Objectivity and the consideration of evidence and alternatives can go out the window. 'Might' is not always 'right', but in 'win–lose' conflicts, might frequently prevails.

Aside from coming to the wrong decision, an outcome of 'win–lose' conflict can be that the 'winner' has their power enhanced and the 'loser' is diminished in some way. The resultant ill-feeling and hostility can mean that the two individuals or groups will find it difficult to trust each other or to work together in the future.

In some cases, the contest can be so intense and damaging that there are no winners; that is 'lose–lose', the classic pyrrhic victory, named after King Pyrrhus of Epirus whose army suffered terrible casualties in defeating the Romans during the Pyrrhic War.

Role of the leader

Authoritative leaders don't ignore conflict, nor do they seek to suppress it. Following the advice of Mary Parker Follett, they seek to resolve it. They don't leave it to the parties concerned to 'sort it out amongst themselves', an example of uninvolved leadership which I've seen at close quarters, and a 'cop-out'. Hopefully, the approach and actions of the authoritative leader will go a long way towards preventing conflict but as has been pointed out, conflict can represent a healthy airing of differing views, and thus the role of the leader is to see the conflict resolved in a 'win–win' fashion for the people and the organisation concerned.

There are a number of approaches or roles for leaders I've observed which parallel the 'win–win' approach to conflict resolution:

- Keep personalities, 'previous records' or history out of discussions.
- Encourage the parties to consider all evidence and options.
- Don't let one party bully the other – give each equal standing and opportunity to express their views; you need to be both coach and referee.
- Be even-handed and open yourself, and be prepared to listen; encourage the individuals or parties concerned to do likewise.
- Focus on the issues and alternatives, encouraging the parties to devise a solution, while keeping in mind that a compromise is often not the best means to accomplish this.
- Be firm and decisive if necessary.
- Adopt a trial period and agree to review any decisions openly after a suitable time.
- Thank the parties for their passion and their contribution.

Flanagan and Finger have offered some simple and helpful advice for coping with irate people, advice that is consistent with 'win–win' approaches and authoritative leadership. I've used this approach successfully in my own work as an educational leader.

As Flanagan and Finger note, letting someone put his or her case is often half the solution to resolving the problem. Sometimes people just want someone to listen:

1. Get the person seated and comfortable (in a suitable location).
2. Listen to what the person has to say.
3. Summarise the situation as you see it.
4. Identify the options.
5. Explore the options and settle on a fair solution.
6. Apportion any blame fairly.
7. Express appreciation.[22]

Finally, let me share a few lessons learned from observing a masterful deputy principal of the 'old school', now deceased, whom I encountered earlier in my career. As a 'year adviser' at a large secondary school, I was often able to observe 'Fred' in action in the DP's office.

Many people tend to be sent to deputy principals for various problems, alleged crimes and atrocities, and 'Fred' dealt with all sorts respectfully, giving every student the chance to put his or her case. He was a 'bushy' by upbringing and alert to the ways of the 'bush lawyer'. He was fair and firm, and guilty students often thanked him when he gave his judgement because of the way he handled the situation.

The lessons I learned were simple yet powerful: that there are always two sides to every story – sometimes more – and you won't find out the truth by making snap judgements. The worst thing you can say is 'I don't want to hear about …'. Another reason for listening is that those students who are 'spinning a yarn' often trip themselves up in their explanations. A final lesson I learned was to distinguish the 'sin from the sinner'; that is, 'You have done a bad thing', rather than 'You are a bad person'. Above all, be fair and respectful, even if you don't particularly admire the person concerned or you find them obnoxious. Keep both your cool and these matters at a professional level.

This also applies to dealing with parents. On occasion, my professionalism has been sorely tested by abusive and in a few cases, drunken parents, including one man who fell off his chair, lay on the floor and wanted to continue his 'interview' from that position. It helps to remember that some people (and their children) have tough lives.

A final comment on conflict

Occasionally you will encounter outright hostility, verbal and physical attacks on persons and total malevolence – what some writers have quaintly called 'nefarious attacks'. This is different to what might be called productive conflict caused by a difference of views. There may be hurtful language, public denigration, defamation, bullying and harassment. People can suffer dreadfully under such attacks.

These situations require a different approach utilising authoritative leadership. Such cases are intolerable and have to be dealt with under the law and according to the regulations and procedures of your school or system. You must act quickly and decisively. An important role for the leader is to protect and defend his or her staff in such situations. You will earn a lot of respect through doing so.

We now move to Chapter 8 which concludes this book.

Notes

1   Duke, D. (2004). *The challenges of educational change* (p. 16). Boston: Pearson.
2   See Glass, G. (2008). *Fertilizers, pills, and magnetic strips: The fate of public education in America*. Charlotte, NC: Information Age Publishing.
3   Janis, I. (1972). *Victims of groupthink*. Boston: Houghton Mifflin.
4   Staw, B. (1976). Knee-deep in the big muddy: A study of escalating commitment to a chosen course of action. *Organizational Behavior and Human Performance*, 16(1), 27–44.
5   Hargreaves, A. (1994). *Changing teachers, changing times* (p. 213). London: Cassell.
6   McLagen, P. (2002). Success with change. *T + D*, December, 44–45.
7   Smith, I. (2005). Achieving readiness for organisational change. *Library Management*, 26(6/7), p. 408.
8   Smith (2005), pp. 408–409.
9   Pennington, G. (2003). *Guidelines for promoting and facilitating change*. York: LTSN Generic Centre. Available at: http://www.heacademy.ac.uk/assets/York/

documents/ourwork/institutions/change_academy/id296_Promoting_and_facilitating_change.pdf
10 From Dinham, S. (2008). Counting the numbers in educational change. *The Australian Educational Leader*, 30(1), 56–57.
11 Dinham, S. (2007). *Leadership for exceptional educational outcomes*. Teneriffe, Qld: Post Pressed.
12 Aubusson, P., Brady, L., & Dinham, S. (2005). *Action learning: What works? A research report prepared for the New South Wales Department of Education and Training*. Sydney: University of Technology Sydney.
13 Dinham, S. (2005). Principal leadership for outstanding educational outcomes. *Journal of Educational Administration*, 43(4), 338–356.
14 Dinham, S. (2007). How schools get moving and keep improving: Leadership for teacher learning, student success and school renewal. *Australian Journal of Education*, 51(3), 263–275.
15 Kotter, J. (1995). Leading change: Why transformation efforts fail. *Harvard Business Review*, 73(2), March-April, 59–67.
16 McBrien, J., & Brandt, S. (1997). *The language of learning: A guide to education terms* (p. 89). Alexandria, VA: Association for Supervision and Curriculum Development.
17 Schein, E. H. (1992). *Organizational culture and leadership*. (2nd ed.). San Francisco: Jossey-Bass.
18 Deal T. E. (1985). The symbolism of effective schools. *Elementary School Journal*, 85(5), 601–620.
19 Zmuda, A., Kuklis, R., & Kline, E. (2004). *Transforming schools* (pp. 18–19). Alexandria, VA: ASCD.
20 Deal, T., & Peterson, K. (1999). *Shaping school culture* (pp. 117–128). San Francisco: Jossey-Bass.
21 See Follett, M. P. (1941). *Dynamic Administration: The collected papers of Mary Parker Follett*. (Henry Metcalf & Lionel Urwick, Eds.). London: Pitman.
22 Flanagan, N., & Finger, J. (1989). *Management in a minute* (pp. 36–37). Brisbane: Plumb Press.

8 | Looking back and moving forward

It is no use saying, 'We are doing our best.' You have got to succeed in doing what is necessary.

(Sir Winston Churchill)

In embarking on the quest to get your school, or your part of a school, moving and improving, it's my experience that when taking over a new role you will probably overestimate what you can achieve in the first 12 months and underestimate what you and your colleagues can achieve in the first three to five years.

Getting moving takes time. I tend to think of one of those large ships that seem to take ages to get up to speed, to change direction and to come to a stop. I'm reminded of a principal who came up to speak with me after I had given a presentation. He explained in a tone of quiet desperation that he had recently taken over as principal at an established primary school with a very experienced staff, most of whom had been at the school for many years. He commented in part: 'I'm the second-youngest member of staff … one of the administrative people is younger. I try to get them to do things and to change but they just ignore me. I think they are waiting for me to go away'.

Some of the successful school leaders I've encountered in research projects and in other contexts have described how their first few years in the role were actually spent going *backwards* – dismantling or reversing certain aspects of their school and its culture before they could get moving in the manner and direction consistent with their vision – essentially throwing the ship into reverse or radically changing direction while simultaneously conducting essential maintenance, no easy or comfortable task.[1] As noted with the principal above, this can prove disheartening, and there has to be at least a small core or critical mass of staff – 'enthusiasts' and 'watchers' – who are willing to support and come with you, because you can't do it on your own.

However, my experience, and those of many of the educators in the studies reviewed in this book, is that the task is achievable, rewarding and even enjoyable. This isn't theoretical speculation or wishful thinking. Schools that were in steep decline – losing students, staff, resources and momentum – were now thriving under the influence of new leadership.* Some had doubled their student numbers as I have noted.

In reading this book, I hope that you have been able to draw from it your own key messages and conclusions that have meaning and value for you in your context and in the years ahead.

However, as well as your own conclusions, the following summary might be useful. You'll be able to recognise that it has been drawn directly from the various research projects canvassed in this book. I haven't committed the researcher's sin of going beyond the data.

If you have been with me all the way until now, you'll know what I am going to say at this point – what follows is not a recipe or formula, but a checklist or framework for reflection, planning, action and evaluation.

Importantly, these phenomena are *outputs* of change as much as *inputs* for further change and improvement, and they take some time and effort to develop.

To begin this overview summary, evidence from my work has convinced me that there are four broad and interdependent fundamentals underpinning student achievement and thus successful schools. These are represented in Figure 8.1 on page 140 and are:

1 a central focus on students, both as learners and people
2 quality teaching
3 professional learning
4 educational leadership.

Putting it all together: How educational leaders get schools moving and improving

How then can we accomplish this task? To unpack the four fundamentals above, it has been demonstrated that the leaders of schools that are moving and improving possess common attributes and adopt similar approaches. Here is a summary:

---

* I have yet to see a 'turn-around' school accomplish this transformation without a change in leadership at or near the top.

```
                    Quality
                    teaching


              FOCUS ON
              THE STUDENT
              (learner, person)


    Leadership                    Professional
                                     learning
```

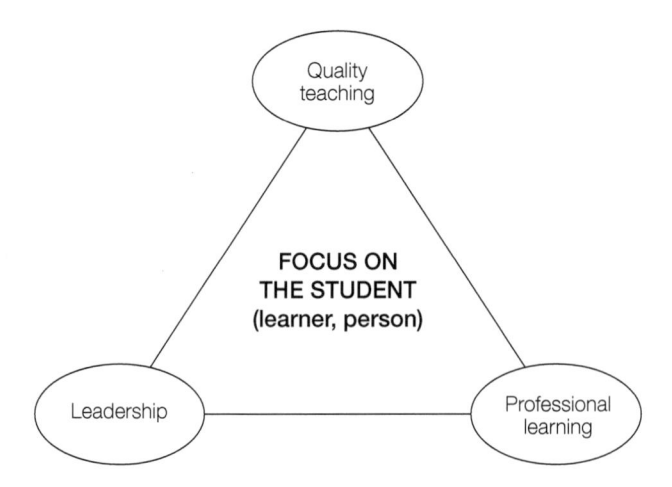

Figure 8.1 The four fundamentals of student achievement

- They make students, as learners and people, the central *focus* of the school.
- They make teaching and learning the central *purpose* of the school.
- They ensure that student welfare policies and programs are integrated with and underpin academic achievement.
- They have a vision of where they want their school to go and of what they want it to be.
- They are effective communicators at all levels.
- They are able to balance the big picture with finer detail.
- They possess perspective and can prioritise.
- They place a high priority on and invest in the professional learning of themselves and others.
- They are informed, critical users of educational research.
- They continually seek to improve the quality of teaching in their school.
- They seek ways for every student to achieve and experience success.
- They act as talent spotters and coaches of talented teachers and release individual and organisational potential.
- They question and push against constraints.
- They seek benefits from imposed change.
- They are informed risk takers and encourage others to do the same.
- They have a positive attitude and seek to drive out negativity.
- They model the values they expect in others such as integrity, altruism and self-growth.
- They build a climate of trust, mutual respect, collegiality and group identity.
- They believe in education for the benefit of the individual and society.

- They work for students, staff, the school and community, rather than for themselves.
- They can read and respond to people and build relationships.
- They have high professional standards and expect high levels of professionalism in return.
- They possess courage and demonstrate persistence and resilience.
- They build productive external alliances with parents, the community, government agencies, business and the profession.
- They entrust, empower and encourage others through distributed leadership and engage in productive team building.
- They provide timely and constructive feedback, good and bad.
- They are approachable and good listeners.
- They create an environment in which people strive to do their best and in which they are recognised for their effort and achievement.
- They emphasise and use evidence, planning and data.
- They are constantly concerned with lifting school performance; nothing is permitted to get in the way.
- They see themselves and their school as being accountable for student achievement.
- Overall, they are authoritative, being highly responsive and highly demanding of individuals, teams and groups, and above all, themselves.

If you can work towards adopting and improving the above practices and developing these attributes, I believe that you will have a very good chance of getting your school moving and improving.

It is NOT a matter of being or not being a born leader, but of being a learner about leadership. I believe that every leader can be a better leader, something that I am also trying to achieve in my own work.

It can't be done alone and the task will not be easy, but the key message is that it *can* be done. To recall one of my favourite quotes from the AESOP study:

> *In this school we make plans now, not excuses.*

I hope that this book will prove helpful in your plans to improve teaching and learning in your school and in the remainder of your career.

Notes

1 See as an example: Dinham, S., Buckland, C., Callingham, R., & Mays, H. (2008). Factors responsible for the superior performance of male students in Years 3 and 5 standardised testing at one Australian primary school. *Curriculum and Teaching*, 23(1), (in press).